THE LEATHER PROTOCOL HANDBOOK

A Handbook on "Old Guard" Rituals, Traditions and Protocols

By Master John, Ftl

John D. Weal

Published by The Nazca Plains Corporation
Las Vegas, Nevada
2010

ISBN: 978-1-935509-76-9

Published by

The Nazca Plains Corporation ®
4640 Paradise Rd, Suite 141
Las Vegas NV 89109-8000

© 2010 by The Nazca Plains Corporation. All rights reserved.
No part of this work may be reproduced or utilized in any form or by any means, electronic or mechanical, including photocopying, microfilm, and recording, or by any information storage and retrieval system, without permission in writing from the publisher. Printed in the United States of America.

Photographer, Jeff Larson
Art Director, Blake Stephens

DEDICATION

The book is dedicated to my Master, may he rest in peace.

To all the leather people I have met throughout my journey, as they have influenced me, molded me, mentored me, befriended me and became my leather family. Without you, there would be no me. Without you, I would not have had the most incredible journey that I ever could imagine. Without you, my life would not have the incredible meaning it has. May you celebrate this book with me, as many of your names are mentioned.

Only you will know who you are by the names used.

To the many boys who have been in my dungeon and taken from me what I had to give them at the time, to the life of education I have done and how it has made me feel complete. Now in my days of being who I am in the world community, I thank all of you who I have met for helping me have the courage and opportunity to write this book.

Thank you one and All as I couldn't have done it without you!

A special thanks to the photographer Jeff Larson for his hours of work in this project.

A special thank you to my model Clayton Naquin. He came into my life through a common friend and volunteered to model for this book. It takes someone special to stand for hours under the lights and constantly pose in the buff and maintain arousal for these hours.

Thank you Clayton!

TABLE OF CONTENTS

FOREWORD BY DR. ROBERT RUBEL	1
PREFACE	2
QUOTE FROM GUY BALDWIN FROM "THE TIES THAT BIND"	4
"OLD GUARD" PROTOCOL – THE HISTORY AND MY JOURNEY	6
ETIQUETTE VS. PROTOCOL VS. RITUAL	27
TYPES OF "OLD GUARD" PROTOCOLS	29
Social Protocol	30
Low Protocol	32
High Protocol	36
"OLD GUARD" RULES AND PROTOCOLS	43
POSITIONS FOR PROTOCOL	61
HAND AND EYE SIGNALS FOR PROTOCOL	68
PROTOCOLS FOR NEGOTIATIONS AND WHAT THEY MEAN	71
DUNGEON PROTOCOLS	73
BOY'S BILL OF RIGHTS	77
LEATHERMAN'S CODES AND CREEDS	79
THE "OLD GUARD" HIERARCHY	81
The Council	81
Elder	82

- Grand Master 82
- Master 83
- Sir 86
- Daddy 88
- Doms 89
- Tops 90
- Boy/boi 90
- slave 96
- Bottom 98

TRAINING OF A BOY IN "OLD GUARD" LIFESTYLES 99
- Behavior in Public 101
- Initial Meeting with a Leather Master, not a Sir 102
- Socializing in Public 105

CEREMONIES 108
- Cover Ceremony 109
- Gauntlet Ceremony 113

COLLARING CEREMONIES 115
- Consideration Collar Ceremony 115
- Training Collar Ceremony 116
- Permanent Collar Ceremony 125
- Slave Collar Ceremony 133

NEW AIRPORT PROTOCOLS 142

NEW GUARD VS NEW LEATHER 148

HANKY CODES 151

IN CONCLUSION 158

ABOUT THE AUTHOR 161

FOREWORD

Those who become interested in the Master/slave structure, whether from within the Leather or the BDSM cultures, almost immediately begin hearing of the "Old Guard." They would hear about Old Guard protocols, ceremonies, and traditions. They also almost immediately get the sense that the Master/slave culture today is based on Old Guard practices, but that there is a certain amount of controversy about exactly which protocols are actually Old Guard and which are modifications of those protocols that have occurred over the decades. They also get the sense that protocols are probably important for their slave(s) but they're not quite sure why they are important.

John Weal has done the M/s community – and the Leather community as a whole – a tremendous service by writing these protocols and ceremonies down in this book. He has done a tremendous service by also explaining why certain protocols were begun in the first place. Reading this book helps people recognize the reasons behind many protocols that are still practiced today. This book is a very valuable resource for us all.

I learned a great deal from John's book. Although I've spent a lot of time researching certain protocols and spoken with a number of seasoned Leather Masters, some of this material was new to me. For example, I had no idea that in Old Guard tradition, Sirs had to earn that title as a step on their path to being recognized as a Master. Similarly, I didn't realize that to become a Sir or a Master, you had to demonstrate a certain number of BDSM skills (such as flogging, or CBT, or...) in order to attain those ranks. No wonder there has always been a certain schism between BDSM and Leather scenes.

Beyond a doubt, through this book you will come to understand more of the history of Leather in ways that may prompt you to incorporate some key aspects of these values, protocols and traditions into your current Leather practices.

Robert Rubel (Dr. Bob)

Dr. Rubel is the author of a four-book set on Master/slave relations, including a book titled: "Protocol Handbook for the Leather slave

PREFACE

First off, I want to state that "Old Guard" life was considered to be only that of gay leather men. This book is about the time when leathermen were exclusive to other leathermen and not into pansexual events and openly sharing our lives with the world. This book is about a time of major change prior to the computer age, the HIV epidemic, the Hep C Virus and the Crystal Meth Crisis and many other changes in the life of gay society. This is not meant to be the end all Bible of gay leather life but strictly an informative book on my personal journey recalling the "Old Guard" protocols, traditions, values, rituals, ceremonies and lifestyle I lived.

Today with the lesbian, transgender, and straight worlds involved in the lifestyles of Leather and BDSM many things have changed. Even our own gay world has changed as we now have rubber men, puppies and many other titles due to the fetish world that has come to be considered under the umbrella of leather life. I do not want to offend anyone in the lifestyle, nor do I want this to be the absolutely only way that people perceive "Old Guard" to be. It is truly just my life and the rituals, traditions and protocols to which I was introduced and lived by and currently understand to be "Old Guard" values.

I hope you enjoy this book and maybe get to understand some things that may make you more aware of what was going on during this incredible time of leather. Hopefully you will understand these "Old Guard" ways and maybe now incorporate some of them into the values, protocols and traditions by which you live your leather life.

The early gay male leather subculture is epitomized by the Leatherman's Handbook by Larry Townsend, published in 1972, which essentially defined one specific order of the Old Guard leather culture. This code emphasized strict formality and fixed roles (i.e. no switching). There is another order of the Old Guard that emphasizes discipline, honor, brotherhood, and respect and promotes an even stricter lifestyle promoting education, knowledge, and privilege based on successive ranks or levels. Leather submissives start as novice trainees and systematically earns their leather while progressing through the levels of third class, second class, first class, and senior trainee. Once a submissive completes his training and earns the senior title, he is ready to go into part time or full time service as a houseboy in an Old Guard Master's household. When gay leathermen cruised in the early 1970s, they began using the bandana code to indicate what kind of sex they were interested in having (some still use the code today).

A true Master or Sir that has been trained in Old Guard, started as a sub and worked his way to his title. Therefore, the Master knows what it feels like to be the sub, knows the pains and the pleasures of that life and is less likely to harm or even kill their sub due to inexperience. This was the way of the "Old Guard". I grew up knowing and which this book is based upon. It was not a myth, but a way of life that promoted many things which have gone from our leather lives today due to the fast growth of our leather community and the quick death of these "Old Guard Men". Some of what you will read may have changed already depending on when you entered the life, if you classify yourself to be "Old Guard". We of course know there was no one way for all leathermen to act. Regions of the country and clubs changed their standards as the times changed, laws changed, and so did the way we met each other due to the internet. I remember when one of the West Coast clubs wouldn't teach fisting as they thought it was too extreme and today fisting is widely taught. It's almost at any venue you attend. We all are evolving, but this is a depiction of what times were like back when our lives started from one leatherman who has survived over 50 years in the lifestyle.

A QUOTE FROM GUY BALDWIN ON "OLD GUARD"
– AUTHOR OF "THE TIES THAT BIND"

"While reading a recent interview with Brian Dawson, I came across some of his comments about that 'Old Guard' in the leather lifestyle. Although I used that label in a piece I wrote almost three years ago, I only recently realized that there was a strong likelihood that large numbers of leather guys don't quite know for sure what the phrase, 'Old Guard' really means. I'm sure that I have never seen a description of the style, and it is a style, so I want to offer one now. I have carried my own 'Old Guard' card in my wallet right next to my Selective Service Registration card (draft card) for long enough that I probably qualify to offer what follows so, here goes...

First, a bit of historical perspective will be more helpful than you might guess. 'Old Guard' is really a misnomer – a misapplied name – for the earliest set of habits that jelled by the mid to late 1950s in the men's leather community here in the U.S. It is very important to remember that the modern leather scene as we now know it first formalized itself out of the group of men who were soldiers returning home after World War II. (l939-1945).

For many gay men of that era, their World War II. military service was their first homosocial experience (first time being thrown together mostly in the company of other men for significant lengths of time), their first time away from their growing up places, and their first experience of male bonding during periods of high stress. War was (and is) serious business; people died, buddies depended on each other for their lives, and the chips were down. Discipline was the order of the day, and the nation believed that only discipline and dedication would win the war and champion freedom: (Ever notice the especially strong patriotic feelings that happen at leather events?)

Anyway, these gay war veterans learned about the value and pleasure of discipline and hard work in the achievement of a noble purpose. They also learned how to play hard when they got the chance for leave time. Indeed, military life during wartime was (and is) a mix of emotional extremes born out of sure knowledge that one could literally be 'here today, and gone tomorrow.' Lastly (for these purposes), the gay vets had the secret knowledge that they fought and served every bit as well as straight soldiers, and this information strengthened their self-esteem. All of these things came to be associated with the disciplined, military way of life as it existed during the wartime years."

A manual of traditional ceremonies, rituals and etiquette.

"OLD GUARD" PROTOCOL –
THE HISTORY AND MY JOURNEY

The US Army's oldest infantry regiment, The "Old Guard", was created on June 3, 1784 as a result of the 1783 Peace of Paris. One of the provisions of the treaty ending the war between Great Britain, France, and the colonies of British America (Americans know the war as the American Revolution) was the requirement that the newly independent colonies take military control and civil responsibility for the land west of the Appalachians. This area is now occupied by the states of Ohio, Iowa, Indiana, Wisconsin, and Michigan, and the border along the Great Lakes with British controlled Canada. At the time, Native Americans and their British allies inhabited this region. This became known as the Battle of Fallen Timbers.

The American army that had won the Revolution (with the help of a French army and French fleet) had been largely disbanded and the troops returned to their respective states in the spring of 1784. The Commander-in-Chief bade good-bye to his officers, and returned to his Virginia farm on the Potomac River. A single, small artillery detachment, posted to West Point, was retained from the Continental Army. For practical purposes, there was no force left to defend the United States. Congress was forced, because of the provisions of the Treaty of Paris, to create an army. The single unit created became The "Old Guard".

The 3rd U.S. Infantry, traditionally known as The Old Guard, is the oldest active-duty infantry unit in the Army, serving our nation since 1784. The unit received its unique name from Gen. Winfield Scott during a victory parade in Mexico City, in 1847, following its valorous performance in the Mexican War. Fifty campaign streamers attest to the 3rd Infantry's long history of service, which spans from the Battle of Fallen Timbers to World War II and Vietnam.

The term "Old Guard" was also used by Napoleon Bonaparte as a means of distinguishing the veterans who had served under him from those that were supporting the new government of 1814. Napoleon graced these veterans with this "Old Guard" nickname as the highest praise possible for their devotion and loyalty to his cause and to France. Upon being exiled to Elba in 1814, these same veterans came to his aid and released him from imprisonment to return him to power until his ultimate defeat at Waterloo.

The "Old Guard" motorcycle troops of the Army, after World War II, were where the history of leather has been documented. As the men came out of the war, the Army awarded them their motorcycles. It was the combination of these wild men renegades wearing leather on their motorcycles, with the BDSM rough-sex men that merged the two names in the late 40's and early 50's so that the term "Old Guard" became attached to the leathermen of BDSM who rode motorcycles. First came the biker bars where motorcycle men would hang out. Next came the renegade bars where men wore basic leather but didn't have motorcycles yet enjoyed rough, wild sex. From those types of bars came the offspring, known as leather bars. Leather bars had started to exist since the early 50's and The Gold Coast, a well-known leather bar in Chicago, where I had my first experiences, opened in the early 60's. Leather life had started to become a reality for us all in our open bars.

I am a leatherman who started on my journey in the late 60's. I became a collared boy in 1968 to a World War II motorcycle man in San Francisco, after meeting him in Chicago. He was the owner of one of the 1940 motorcycles that was given to him for his war service as an "Old Guard" motorcycle man. He remained in San Francisco after the war, starting his leather journey with some of the other men from the war. These men missed the camaraderie they had when they were in the military as well as the strict way of life, so they had formed a club. Out of that club, grew what I knew to be the "Old Guard" leather culture that incorporated rigid order and rules with a new member being apprenticed to a more experienced member. It was with that club I became a member of "Old Guard" culture.

Upon being collared, Master and I lived in the Castro district of San Francisco during the time of Harvey Milk and the gay rights movement. Harvey Milk was assassinated November 27, 1978. We all marched in the Candlestick March in his memory as he had done so much for our gay rights as well as for our leather rights in San Francisco. It was a major time of change for gay rights. This was a time when Leather was going through changes as well but was yet in the closet for most gay men. The motorcycle men had reputations of fear and humiliation, which really wasn't the case but like many stereotypes, the few make the many look bad.

The main and number one code at that time was not to scare the villagers as leathermen. We needed to work on being accepted even in our gay society. Our sex lives were classified taboo, freaky and we as leathermen were looked at as being dangerous. In fact, if you were found to be in possession of anything denoting BDSM by police you stood a chance of being put in jail. The "Old Guard" was a community that valued privacy, and not without reason; there are numerous instances where people who practiced S&M were jailed or committed to psychiatric hospitals for their choices and actions. As late as 1990, police busted a private group in Dorchester near Boston Ma. While it is not even certain that there were any prosecutions, all of the participants names were published in the local press and most of the men involved lost their jobs; one even committed suicide.

This was why secrecy was critical. People still remembered the Nazi Pink Triangle that denoted the homosexuals that were put into concentration camps and put to their death. We lived in so much fear. Harvey was freeing us so much from those fears until his death. We all really felt his death, as he was one who stood up for us all and our rights and wasn't afraid. He opened our gay eyes as well as our leather eyes to step forth and not be so afraid. He impelled us all to become open and fight for our rights. In my eyes he was a true leader and should never be forgotten in gay history and yes our leather history.

Master was a medical doctor from the service and we lived a very open life to our leather friends, but sheltered from the world, as the world of leather was private during those times shared only by like people in the lifestyle. Everyone in the lifestyle was sworn to secrecy about each other as well as to uphold the secret ways of our club. No one talked outside of the circle of friends about anything leather.

To enter the lifestyle you had to be networked into the club. You were then screened heavily by various members of the club prior to even being exposed to the club. It was there where you were first introduced to the play parties and runs. The parties and runs were very private and really non-consenting acts would happen, not as they are today. Many things were done out of excitement and fun with no concern in many cases for the safety or health of anyone involved. Sexually the only things we had to worry about then were gonorrhea and syphilis, which could be cured by a shot. Maybe crabs but that was the least of our worries. It was all about torture for sexual pleasure and a life of service to our style of living. Passion was present with a deep seeded hidden value of trust. What we did wasn't thought of as kinky but as perverted and not normal by society standards. We lived in serious fear of being found out. I witnessed many things which today would be either not accepted or even considered something where someone would be put in jail. Regardless of how we see it now, we cannot change the facts, that is was what happened back in the early years.

Some of the practices would be classified as abuse today and totally not in the realm of reality by many. For us, it was the way we lived. We lived to protect one another. We accepted it to be part of the group. No questions were asked. If people were hurt, we surrounded them and cared for them so no one saw what had happened until they healed. It was a very different time, but with respect and trust for one another. I can only describe it as it built integrity, stamina and loyalty, not out of want, but out of fear for what might happen to us if you didn't. This was my way of life in what I called "Old Guard" for the early years of my life in service. It was what I knew to be the only way to live; a valued way of life based upon trust and community where we all would put our trust in one another, in our clubs and local community to protect each of us. I'm sure you have heard the expression "all for one and one for all". This is how we lived.

Today people yearn for the knowledge of what we did and why we did it. It was a time where jeans, boots and leatherjackets were our daily attire. Our leathers were primitive, ranging from brown to black and they were never bought but usually handmade by a friend who showed some leather craftsman talents. Our toys were primitive, yet things were developing and changing faster than one could keep track of then. Life as we knew it was about to go into fast forward with diseases, death, computers, social changes, free love, money and many other things about to explode in our lives as leathermen and the world.

Play parties were private and held in private places where no one would find us and not on a regular basis so they would never be found out. It was done by word of mouth with no written invitations. We had our Elders, Grand Masters, Masters, Sirs, Daddies and tops with boys and slaves. Puppies were not even in our thoughts at that time yet they would soon emerge. Computers were only things thought about by men with a vision of a future life. It was a tight knit community and you were accepted only by being brought in by someone who knew you.

To be brought into the group, you were drilled in front of the fellow men of the group. Much like in a tight fraternity, this was the way things were. Because of this the groups/clubs became very exclusive rather than inclusive, meaning that the people in the scene and clubs understood the rules, traditions and privacy needed. Trust needed to instilled and earned. We all tried to keep the outsiders out. An outsider was defined as a gay man, butch or not, who did not have a primary interest in experiencing the erotic BDSM sexualities involved along with the protocols. They had to at least have an interest in motorcycles. That exclusion attitude we all possessed was inevitably reinforced by the guilt about being kinky and liking it that way. Back then we were not openly considered part of the gay community. We were outcasts even to our very own. We were feared by the gay men and we were afraid the gay men would out us so we were not in unity at this point of our life. Fear of jail, outing our self, and the entire lifestyle was at stake for each and every one of us.

Life was about to explode. Toys were about to become things that were readily available in adult bookstores. Leather stores were not in existence anywhere and had yet to evolve into existence. You earned your leathers by your deeds and community status; you didn't just buy them. Life as a leather person was not something people would proclaim. We hid it as if we were ashamed of it. Much like the time when gay people would seek out other gay men by asking if you were "friends of Dorothy", we would use code words to find and network to gay life. Leathermen would seek out other leathermen based upon their looks and attire. In fact there used to be a saying that leathermen would use to find out about other leathermen and that was "do you play a saxophone or mandolin?" The saxophone player was the sadist and the mandolin player was the masochist. As you can see things were very different in those early years. Almost every word spoken was in some sort of code so as not to reveal what you were or what you were seeking. Every word was to protect you from society as a whole including our fellow gay brother.

Motorcycle bars were the start of leather bars as leather was worn as a means of protection against harm on the bike should an accident occur. These bars also had the very masculine men, which is why leather took on the masculine persona. We would go there to seek out gay masculine men and then break out to have our sexual activities.

Based on the men dancing with men only environments of the 1800's, men wore different colored handkerchiefs to denote who was the male and who was the female. Hanky colors filtered into the leather life as another way of helping us to define what we sought. The initial hanky colors denoted not male and female but tops (which were more or less the butch men) and bottoms (not saying they are female but the receivers), helping us find our own. Where we wore these hanky colors became which position we preferred. Soon hanky colors became part of our culture to dictate what we sought and the type of fetish we sought. Based on that culture, leathermen were making it easier for our leather tribes to find one another or to find men with similar play needs. We still needed to be careful of the hanky colors as people soon became aware of what they meant. We were still in the closet, so to speak, protecting our lives so many times the hankies didn't come out until we got to our bars.

Our bike keys also played a part at this point as to whether or not we were looking for sex or not looking for sex. We would wear them in certain positions denoting not only top and bottom but also their location on the side denoted whether we were looking or not looking. Hidden keys meant rough sex. See the hanky colors later in this book for the various meanings of the hanky colors. You will also find what positions of the keys were and what they their locations meant. The hanky colors listed are what they mean today as the hanky color code has greatly expanded from the basic colors we wore in "Old Guard". There were only four colors back then black for heavy s/m, Grey for heavy bondage, green for Daddies, yellow for water sports. Red was quickly introduced for fisting and ass play shortly after I became involved in the lifestyle. Oh I remember the controversy over the addition of red hankies. There were those that felt that the red hanky was way too pronounced and caused too much attention and was sometimes confused with the bandanas the cowboys wore as it was pretty well known in the country western lifestyle back then. Could it be misread by one of our fellow leathermen and have us outed because we chose to pick up a country western man who was straight?

Motorcycles seemed to be our mode of travel and for most of us a major part of our common bond. We couldn't talk of play parties so we talked about our bikes and our trips and only those on those bike runs would know what went on. This is how our sexual events became named runs, as they were actually our rides out of town for sex. We would run out of the streets of San Francisco on our bikes, out to some God forsaken beautiful area or some abandoned place to play. This is also how we got to be known as the renegades and the wild ones as people would only imagine what went on and really thought we were rotten nasty men who were rough and crude and perverted far beyond anyone's imagination. We wouldn't have sex in our homes but outside and in bizarre places such as abandoned factories and warehouses and the wharfs. There is where their imaginations would run wild about what went on and how many people were involved. It was their own vivid imagination of what went on that gave us the bad names. If people only knew how wonderful it all seemed and how great the men really were. But we wanted the persona to keep our distance from the main sector.

Yes there were numbers of men but it wasn't always passing around time and everyone did everyone else. I am also not saying there wasn't some of that as well. Publicly was one image and personally I can tell you they were warm wonderful intense masculine men who knew what they wanted and were not afraid to take or give it. As I stated earlier, that my mind reminisces on some of the most wonderful play parties I personally attended. But those were the days and we didn't have the sexual infections and issues of today, so things could happen that can't or shouldn't happen now.

Tribes were now being formed based on various likes and dislikes. Many tribes were formed across the United States giving birth to different protocols, etiquettes, and rituals, which differed from tribe to tribe, and life spread with the views of many people changing the way leather was perceived. But the original tribes of leathermen in San Francisco were more structured and remained so as our lives spread across the United States and Europe. These men believed in the structure, strictness and stability of what they stood for. It provided us new men something to follow and be trained at. Something we could count on. The three "S's" of leather life. These rules and protocols along with the rituals and traditions varied by club but mostly there were a lot of basic things that existed in most clubs. Protocols that were not that hard to learn and not that difficult to remember were followed. The codes of ethics and protocols came mostly from the military where they existed daily. Many of the men had relied on those protocols in their military life and missed them now in their civilian life. They were revived and applied to the club life we all knew.

In the mid-1960s, classic leather styles began to give way to a kind of "hippie leather." People grew their hair, took psychedelic drugs, became less invested in 1950s formality and created new subgroups organized around different sexual styles, for example fistfucking. At one point, dope smoking leather guys and fistfuckers were in effect a kind of "New Guard," although that terminology was not yet commonly used.

The expansion of leather life through Europe added another side to the leatherman's life and that was the use of Nazi uniforms. In the beginning, many motorcycle leathermen had issues with this due to the fact that the enemy they killed wore these Nazi uniforms. These Nazi men in the war were also the ones who put us in concentration camps and killed us. For many of us "Old Guard" men this was a mental block. How could this come into our leather life? It represented the institution that we had fought in many ways. Through all this Tom of Finland artwork emerged into leather life. Tom portrayed this ultra masculine man with an enormous cock. Leathermen were drawn to Tom's images in our fantasies. Tom eventually drew the Nazi uniform as well as other hot men in other styles of military uniforms such as sailor uniforms. He used the Nazi uniform from the demanding Hitler and put it on the dominant man in these pictures. Soon it became accepted in leather life as a sign of Hitler's power over his troops or men. The sign of power being the key words here over his men!

This in turn led to our military uniforms being introduced into the Tom of Finland artwork. Once we had our military uniforms, the Nazi uniforms soon became a uniform of choice for dominant men. It also represented strictness, which was also part of Hitler's discipline and his rise to power. This resonated straight to the hearts of leathermen. It soon came through in leather as a power uniform, a dominant Master/Sir/top's uniform. Today all types of uniforms including police and firemen are being worn by leathermen.

The erotic art of Tom of Finland happened and was now here to stay in our leather life. Tom and all his sexy men were representatives of all the uniforms, centered around Tom in his Leathers, which now gave uniforms their validity in our leather life. The incredible masculine men filled all of our fantasies about those hot military times during the war.

Leather life was evolving as fast as was gay life. Life was more open than we ever knew possible then, but still so closeted compared to now. Tom of Finland represented so much more to us than erotic art; he in many ways was the man we all yearned to be physically. Even today the muscle men of leather are still some of the hottest looking men in leather. It has become the ultimate look in leather but that doesn't mean they are the ultimate players in the BDSM leather lifestyle. And so the look of leather versus the leather men who play in the BDSM lifestyle begins to happen.

Hot men however don't necessarily mean physically only. It depends on the person interpreting the hotness. Each of us has different tastes in men which makes it hot for all of us and for that reason, I am thankful. I am one who is not a muscleman. However, I do like to have a boy/boi/submissive/slave with some muscle as they can endure more from me. That is my thought process anyway. I also have learned that isn't necessarily true either. It just happens to be my fantasy and my preference.

There are many who think I am hot because I am a big massive dominant man who is educated in leather and is knowledgeable of our "Old Guard" lifestyle. So you see there is someone for everyone in leather. Don't let your personal image discourage your journey as I have found out this is a very true statement. I am always amazed at who and what I attract as there have been some really great musclemen as well as some nicely toned boys who submit to me and other boys who are not but have incredible minds and can endure a lot which can turn me on also. It is all about the chemistry and energy we share and that should be what we all seek. Physique, mind, shape, cock, ass, body type and physical aura all determine that. I think you will find all that to be true and really true when you finally connect with that Master/Sir or boy/boi/submissive/slave.

Let's get back to the time line. In the mid-1960s, the age of free love came to be our next era. We exploded through the woodwork, accepting people of all genders and lifestyles. Sex became experimental along with drugs. Leather life spread like wildfire because drugs seem to give people the ability to go falsely into sub space and break down the barriers giving people freedom to play, doing things they wouldn't normally do. This widened our spectrum of sex and our abilities to do many other things. Free love, as it was known, became a time of sexually active people doing sex anonymously and with strangers, uninhibiting our sexual desires, opening up yet another world in leather. We no longer did it with the just men we knew. It widened our anonymous sexual desires for strange men and instant gratification with those hot men. We now were having sex everywhere in public bathrooms and just about any place one could. Even airport bathrooms were fair game. A toe tapping under a stall would soon result in a hot sexual encounter.

By the mid-1970s, there were several distinct leather styles and cultures, although individuals could move among them. After Stonewall, and I hope you all know what I mean by the Stonewall Riots, the urban gay male populations came out of the woodwork, and by the late 1970s leather had become a kind of uniform for urban gay men – most of whom would never experience the actual feeling from the end of a whip. This "clone" look included short haircuts, mustaches, tight 501 jeans, boots, leather jackets, and keys dangling from belts.

The late 1970s are often seen as a kind of "golden age" of SM in San Francisco, but the large-scale adoption of leather styles by non-leathermen diluted the signals and frustrated the hard-core leather population. This situation led to the founding of the 15 Association in 1980. The 15 intended to create a more reliable SM environment, in which people did not wear hankies or keys as fashion accessories. However, even today the 15 Association does embrace all that they set out not to embrace just like every other BDSM club has done. Funny, how life has the tendency to do this. It is very hard to stay true to your original thoughts and beginnings as life demands so much more of each of us and as our clubs grow.

Women became part of our lifestyles in the 70's at a great speed. The dikes on bikes began to form and soon their culture took the same paths as our men previously and we soon began to accept them into our life. I remember the first time I saw a woman on a bike: I laughed and said who is she trying to be? Well now I have come to respect women in leather as they have proven their part in our history and taken to our sides when we were down in numbers and stood by our sides as we died. Many of those older women have seen many of us "Old Guard" men pass on and have heard the stories of our lives on our death beds holding our hands taking care of us and have taken those stories to their graves. God bless them. My cover is off to them and now I welcome them as I do anyone into our life, but during those early years it was really funny watching women emerge into the life. Now some of them are even meaner then the men I have come to know. They have earned the right to wear the leather in my book for their contribution to the lifestyle.

In the late 70's early 80's, "the gay cancer" began to emerge which caused most of us to go back into the closet, protecting everything we stood for. Through the 80's we lost most of the tribes in San Francisco as well as worldwide. We were losing our heritage so fast that we would see one of our fellow leathermen and two weeks later they were gone either from the disease or in fear of the disease by taking their own lives once they were infected. Leathermen rallied hard to help stop this disease as most of our brothers were infected due to the wild crazy sex parties and other activities that were going on in our dungeons. Leather folk still are one of the strongest supporters of fighting HIV and funding its research for this very reason. But during this time we lost most of our heritage and our background. So much was lost that "Old Guard" was at risk. People were entering our lifestyle through the drugs and sex and looseness of our bodies under the influence. Our secrets were leaking out or dying. How would we ever hold on to this life we knew and treasured?

Shortly after the 70's, became the era of Titles and Title holders. They would represent the community and try to promote good will and promote the hotness of leather. They wore the leathers we all wore. Yes, they did look hot in them but there was a saying that the pretty men in leather really never knew what it was like to experience the end of the whip. Their wearing black leather clothing was an erotic fashion that expresses heightened masculinity or the appropriation of sexual power. It could also have meant their love of motorcycles and independence. Rarely did it mean their engagement in sexual kink or leather fetishism. The first well known contest was Mr. Gold Coast Leather from Chuck Renslow the owner of the famed Chicago gay leather bar called The Gold Coast. In 1979 Chuck Renslow turned Mr. Gold Coast Leather into International Mister Leather as his dream grew from a local contest to be an international contest for hot men. Chuck created this contest partially out of his own sexual desires for these hot men from all over the world as well as his desires to grow this contest to be one of the biggest in the world. His dream continued to grow. Now in 2010, celebrating 32 years, we have our first transgendered leathermen to win the contest! Following this contest we then had the Mr. Drummer contest which changed names to become the International Leather Sir/boy contest due to some legal issues. There were many issues, but one was from the motion picture industry where it was said our symbol resembled the Oscar symbol and we had to change it. It was to be the real players contest and title, to give us both the beauty and the beast so to speak; the real leather BDSM men and the pretty, hot men of leather for International Mister Leather. It was in 1986 that Tony DeBlase (better known as Fledermaus in the leather community and publisher of Dungeon Master) and his partner Dr. Andrew Charles moved from Chicago, IL to San Francisco, CA and purchased the Drummer magazines from Alternate Publishing. Drummer thrived under DeBlase's passionate direction, reaching their peak in power and influence by the time they were sold in 1992. In 1988, the publisher of Drummer and also the owner of the Mr. Drummer contest, Tony DeBlase moved the contest from Gay Pride in June to late September to coincide with the Folsom Street Fair, creating "San Francisco Leather Pride Weekend," a six day calendar of leather and SM events. This is still looked at as one of the biggest events in the United States and the World. People from all over the world come now to attend this weekend in San Francisco. It is because of this huge success the world of BDSM and leather culture has come to mean so much for so many. Few know how much they depended on DeBlase for their success in some way.

There were some issues however for Tony DeBlase and Drummer Magazine. It was particularly poor timing on their part. AIDS, of course, was decimating the population, which was a significant chunk out of the leather community. Censorship had just started again badly. The Meese Commission Report had just come out. S & M was the most taboo thing that most people were considering. And while there was no formal censorship, there was informal censorship, in that the distributors that they counted on to buy and distribute the magazines were intimidated by it. They didn't want the local District Attorney, who wanted to make a name, come in and find this on their shelves, or in their warehouses. And so they would cancel. If the Drummer magazine had a picture in the magazine that they didn't like, there went several hundred copies down the drain. Of course, you didn't find that out until after they had paid to have those several hundred copies printed. Drummer also discovered that one of the problems of the magazine business is all of your expenses are expected to be paid upon delivery or prior to delivery, whereas all of your income from major distributors comes 120 days after they've received shipment, have sold what they can, and returned the rest to you, and they pay only for those that they sold. This was not a sound financial environment or a good business venture. In the words of the great Tony DeBlase, "It was not a good time for us, not a good time at all."

It was during the earthquake in San Francisco October 17, 1989, that all was lost for the Drummer Magazine and the building in which it was housed. Again more of our history lost forever. As the late Tony DeBlase said "We had no insurance as only residences were able to carry earthquake insurance" and "it was just too costly to start up the publication back to what it was". They walked away from the building turning the mortgage back to the mortgage holder. The Magazine faltered until 1992 when it was sold.

Both International Mister Leather and the International Leather Sir/boy contest have grown to great magnitudes and have over 18,000 leather folk at an event. Who would ever have guessed it? Contests continued to grow until now we have Mr. somebody from every city and county almost everywhere in the U.S. and abroad. I am also proud to state we have added International Bootblack to both contests and International Miss Leather better known as IMsL to these great events broadening our scope. There are also many other International Fetish titles which I won't address as I am an "Old Guard" Leatherman but they are part of our culture today and growing each year as well.

In the beginning of these contests, when the contestants were questioned about leather life and who, what, when and where, they had no knowledge of many things. They lost some respect with this lack of knowledge from many leathermen, though they were hot and looked hot, they turned some of us off. They just became good will ambassadors trying to help us gain recognition in our gay community and for that we would respect them. Now in the contests, judges started to do question and answer segments so they could find out more about these contestants. Did they have any real fetishes? Why were they wearing leather? Questions about our leather history. Today, we still have some contestants who just enjoy wearing leather and that is ok, but more and more they are beginning to start to understand there are choices in their journey here. They find out about "Old Guard" men who open up their views and knowledge to continue their leather journey. They may not embrace it and live it but at least they are knowledgeable about "Old Guard". Having the knowledge now gives them a choice in how they choose to live in leather and now other fetishes.

Questions about leather history instead of just their cock sizes were now are being asked. Soon questions arose about our boots and what they meant and various questions on our boots. Bootblacks were in our bars now keeping our boots clean. Our boots soon became a large part of our fetish. Bootblacks were added to these contests. As leathermen, we needed to recognize them, as boots were so much part of our lives.

One of the reasons why contests have yet to fully gain "Old Guard" respect is the lack of proper protocol during these contests and at other leather events. Even a simple thing like the introduction of titleholders' finds most producers and event coordinators at a loss as to what is appropriate.

"Old Guard" protocols and the leather movement itself stemmed out of a military model. Part of the "trust and respect" we frequently speak of is based on this model. Military men were trained to trust their fellow man as well as respect their fellow man in battle. Also just good old fashioned manners. Too often contest producers and event coordinators fail to implement these basic ideals into their programming. The result is an all too often haphazard attempt at introductions without any set standard. At a recent "major" city contest, producer's failed to introduce current International titleholders three times during their event weekend! Without a set standard in place, these introductions become subjective and not based on factual information for which "Old Guard" values are based upon.

As a rule or guide, current International titleholders should always be introduced first followed by the current national, regional, state, city and then bar titles. Following these introductions then would come the past international title holders, national, regional, state, city and then bar titles all in the order in which they received their titles. The exception to this rule is the introduction of a Head Judge, which should come at the beginning of the contest introductions. Bootblack Titleholders' should be included in this simple and fair method, as they too are not always defined by just one orientation. This method mirrors the standards that are based in military rank, and places the status on one's title year i.e. International 2009 title holders would come before international 2008, 2007, 2006. The subsequent years would be after the current Mr. Oklahoma 2009, Mr. Tulsa 2009 then Mr. Tulsa Eagle 2009. Following these would then come oldest to newest International title holders followed by the oldest to newest regional state, city, and bar and so on. The Oldest to Newest would be used as the Oldest would carry more weight much like a senior officer in the military. The newer title holders would not be as seasoned or knowledgeable therefore, giving way to their elder. Then we would also have to add "Old Guard" male first female would be second with non gender being third for example. International Mister leather 2009, International Master 2009, International Sir 2009, International Miss leather 2009, International boy 2009, International Bootblack 2009, International slave and so on. International Bootblack and slave come last due to they are non gender and orientation specific (Master, Sir, Dom, Mr. and Ms).

How can we possibly obtain the information on when each individual titleholder received their current title? The answer is quite simple; just ask them or have them write it down on a sign-up sheet prior to the event. This way no one person is left out, forgotten, and the many that still value Old Guard protocols will be satisfied by the attempt. It also gives the event producers time to organize it and put it in proper order and not forget to recognize anyone if they have signed in. This makes it not the event or producer's fault but the titleholder's fault if they didn't register their name.

I began to notice some other shifts in the mid-1980s, when the energy at public play parties seemed to change for the worse. Before then, many of the parties had been informal rituals of solidarity, pleasure, celebration, and connection. People used to care mostly about having a good time. Even in casual or recreational play, the focus seemed to be on the quality of the connection between the players themselves and on building and sharing energy that whole rooms could get high on together. At some time in the mid-1980s, it seems that many people began to care more about what the audience saw than what their partners experienced. Leather had become trendy and popular rather than despised and stigmatized. Others seemed to merely go through the motions – SM has too often become a mechanical exercise rather than an art form or a form of intimate communication. I'm not saying that there is no great public play today, but I often see a community that lacks some of its former style, grace, and values as well as the strictness, structure and stability around which we had built our lives.

In 1992, AOL 1.0 was released. AOL introduced the first email services and life was now about to change dramatically for all of us. Computers had both a positive and negative effect on our culture as suddenly we had a way to network worldwide to contact other members of tribes and friends that we made along the journey. Soon web locations, chat rooms and runs began to pop up all over the world with everyone adding their own rules. People found out about the lifestyle, wanting this way of life, changing it to fit their individual needs.

Computers made it possible for people to chat behind a false persona allowing them to express themselves freely, giving them even more freedom. Computers also gave us the ability to go worldwide behind these disguises and freedoms, spreading truths and falsehoods about our lives. However you look at it, it did give us this total acceptance and non-judging environment. People suddenly became self-taught experts who really didn't have any knowledge of the former leather life. It gave them self-confidence to make believe they were somebody in a world of computers where they never would have to prove anything to anyone. However, using these disguises also allowed people to find out who they themselves were, which brought more people into our lifestyle. Computers also gave them the ability to do research and learn, which gave serious seekers that avenue of education. So you see, it wasn't all bad, it certainly helped make some of the great people today, who they are. I know many leathermen who have achieved a lot of their education from different websites. They in turn however sought out the clubs and became thriving active members. At least this is my belief.

A footnote for all you self-proclaimed people: Where is the "I" in Master or slave? I once had a conversation with someone online and they said to me I don't care about "Old Guard", I want it when I want it, where I want it, and how I want it. Forget the protocols and codes it's going to be what I want. I am the Master. Wow! Can you imagine how I felt talking to this person? Who was he? He had no knowledge of anything or any education. He was just some self-proclaimed "Master" wanting it only his way with no regards to anything but his own personal desires. How long would he last or how long would it be before he hurt someone. Well life was changing and I found how much and how fast it was changing with this conversation.

Along with the computer however, came danger. People didn't have the training or background we had all earned and worked so hard to protect. They didn't know what the titles meant or how we had to work to earn them, so they awarded themselves titles, which were undeserved, and soon people were getting hurt. Because of this lack of knowledge, today people are still being hurt. We are slowly gravitating back to "Old Guard" ways, as people are learning there was an art and talent to being a great dominant. When I hear someone in the New Guard try to use the word "Master or Sir," my skin sometimes crawls. The word is not a name or a noun in my world. It cannot be used as if it were. It is a title, a deference, a display of earned respect, and can only replace a name in direct conversation with the respected party. The New Guard likes the word, feels the energy charge in it and, apparently, mistakes the energy charge for the substance.

Bottoms, boys and slaves are also learning there is a reason why they need to be educated. They need to understand the headspace and the traditions of why they desire to serve. People worldwide are learning there was a reason for the progression of titles. There is a need for training and education. This is why people who have joined our lives, seek the history. Training and education is on a worldwide surge. Yes we have many more people in the life and yes I believe it will all work its way out but, the structure, strictness and stability is still being craved.

Now in the XXI century, we are facing yet additional epidemics in gay life as a whole. They are Crystal Meth and the Hep-C epidemics which again are changing the way we play and the way in which we share our lives as leatherfolk. People are dying from these epidemics as well as from AIDS and once again the leather community is trying to support and help these individuals. We rally around these people offering support both financially and mentally, helping them through this new crisis too. It is up to each of us to help our fellow leathermen or leatherwomen in their journeys. Today we need to support them in whatever way we can, infected or not by any of these epidemics.

Apart from increases in numbers, popularity, and commercialization, the gay leather community has had to deal with one really unique factor that cannot be underestimated: the escalated rate of early mortality due to AIDS, Hep C and Crystal Meth. The HIV/AIDS epidemic has damaged leather communities and social life in incalculable ways. Communities have experienced great loss. In a short period of time, communities have experienced the great loss of many of the men (and quite a few women) who made major contributions to creating and sustaining the public leather life we once knew. Now with Hep C and Crystal Meth even more are dealing with this mortality issue and even greater numbers of people are dying losing even more than we know and our history.

I luckily survived the HIV epidemic. I have come to be the last living member of our club and the stories that I will talk about, as well as the protocol, etiquette and rituals are my contribution to preserving those early years and times. I will talk about it all shortly but know that if you choose to use it you honor me and if you choose to not honor me at least you know about it and that too makes me proud to do what we are about to do together.

The collective absence of so many leather forebears is, I think, one of the main reasons why the social changes of the last decade seem to have produced so much more of a chasm than did previous ones. These people not only built and refined our institutions, but they also met and talked and played with innumerable others, all the while transmitting community values to newcomers. Their loss has damaged the social fabric of the leather community and has created huge gaps in the transmission of leather culture and history. Some of this culture and history has been irretrievably lost forever, and our leather society today has had to reinvent important pieces of itself as a result. I believe this is the principle reason why "Old Guard" and New Guard have such differences. This is the reason why I have been asked to write about what I witnessed and lived and what you will soon read.

Although much has been lost, as gay leather/BDSM has evolved, new developments have brought positive changes as well as new problems. I'm not proposing that we could or should go back to the 1950s. I also believe we should neither romanticize the past nor fail to value it. Today, there are many ways to acquire leather attitudes and leather knowledge, including open classes, events, books, the Internet, and structured programs, as well as more valued true traditional apprentice relationships. Many people are realizing we need to value what was good and they are seeking out these stories, traditions, and ceremonies. They are trying to regain the values adding once more the strictness, structure and stability that once was so vital and critical to our way of life. They realize the need and are today trying to reinstate those values and weed out the bad ones but understand why they were there. As well as why we had to change them, yet not forget them.

Today New Leather or New Guard and all the acronyms out there including the Vanguard are from when the computer age arrived and the years that followed in my opinion. Life as we all know it today in the 2010's again is changing dramatically. I just returned from IML 2010 and we have a transgendered titleholder holding the title of International Mister Leather.

It is for these reasons I have been asked to write this book and tell everyone the stories that go with my life as a true "Old Guard" leatherman. It is why I believe before I die, educating and training people in the lifestyle and the history I lived are a worthwhile journey for me. I hope you will read this book with all the tears, passion, respect and understanding of what was once a way of life I knew, craved and protected. A way of life which I am asked about daily, even just to reminisce of a life long ago when I met Master to his passing away. Yes, it is in my blood and yes, I feel my heart beat when I play and meet "Old Guard" leathermen in my journeys.

As I have retired now, it has become my whole life, a sort of return to my roots, enjoying my life, sharing in its wonders and ways with those of you who wished you could have lived during that time. Yes it was an incredible time for me and it can be for you if you embrace it. But to embrace it is to love it. Put your mind, heart, soul and body in it. There is no reason why you and your clubs, partners, play partners, mentors, and friends can't live in traditions of "Old Guard". Who knows in years to come, you may be in the same position and writing of your life with a different yet symbolic meaning close to mine sharing with the world your feelings and knowledge remembering mine and how it influenced you. And if you do, know that you have not only honored me and my life but all the leather men and women before you who have embraced that life.

It is indeed a wonderful journey for us all to live. Live it to your fullest capabilities, be it "Old Guard", New Guard or Vanguard. I remember Master recalling a line which comes from a famous old 1950's Broadway show called "Auntie Mame", "Life is a banquet and most poor sons of bitches are starving to death. So Live! Live! Live!" No truer words were ever spoken in my eyes. This line was later changed to be in the movie "Life is a banquet and most poor suckers are starving to death", now voted one of 100 best lines from a movie.

I know famous leathermen, who will say that "Old Guard" today is just the way things were then. It's a myth. There was no one way things were done. This for the most part is true. Just as today will be "Old Guard" to people 30 years from now and with all the clubs who really knows what's going on if we don't document it. I can understand that theory and can agree to it somewhat, but I must say It wasn't a myth and certainly wasn't to me. There were some basics that were pretty much followed by most of the groups, clubs or tribes. Some of the forms are genuine and have history, but they never had the kind of universal acceptance and weight they are given in "memory."

That is not a problem! If inventing a way of life that is loosely based on the behaviors of the "Old Guard" results in a myth that can breathe and have value in the lives of leathermen today, let it happen. "If Sy Lechter, Jim Kane, Bill Swenning and Val Martin are to be made gods in a pantheon they would not recognize, I don't think they would have a problem with it. Better to become giants and myths than to be ignored and forgotten forever". These were words of one well-known leatherman and I agree. And much of what is being created in the name of the "Old Guard" is genuinely useful, regardless of how it is rooted in the past.

Is there really a New Guard/"Old Guard"/ Vanguard conflict? Yes, absolutely! What's more, I believe there will always be a conflict between the forces driving us through our leathersex and leather-social road. Personally, I can be very nostalgic for the rigid strict simplicity of the small, tightly networked groups of the BDSM men I first came to know. I liked the freedom that came from everyone knowing all we needed to know about everyone. The fellowship they observed, their mannerisms and attitudes, the forms of respect which they used. I liked the signs and displays of submission. I enjoyed the three "S" of "Old Guard", Strictness, Structure and Stability as well as the easy acceptance of a superior place and those special men. But these are all part of the now, the nearly lost side, and the traditional men known as the ""Old Guard"." I truly lived this life and can tell you of my life over the past 42 years. Be it "Old Guard" to you or just an old man's memory of the way things were, it truly was a way of life that is lost.

I believe there are many reasons why we are the people and tribes we are today. Yes there were some things that needed to be protected and yes there were things, which I will state, were wrong and needed to be corrected. I also know that life has changed dramatically. With HIV, Hep C and Crystal Meth plus all the other diseases out there as well as just plain danger in serious play, we all have to take responsibility for whom and what we do. I hope that with the respect of what you may learn from me or from any other "Old Guard" protocol handbook, you will cherish it and take from it at least the history that has made us who we are today and pass on those stories, traditions, protocols and etiquette so the meaning of that life isn't lost.

Much like the documentation of our country's history and the different stories that exist there, this is just one more telling to document that time when life was different. Hopefully when you finish this book some things will make sense from some of the stories you have heard. Hopefully you will now honor some of these traditions, protocols, and etiquette in your leather tribe/family/organization and find the meaning for why they existed. Maybe you will believe in them and understand what it meant to me and my family, tribe and organization. Maybe you may even adopt some of them into your life or tribe, club or community. I know this: if you do you will find that the three "S's" will help you give your relationship, club, tribe and community just what they stand for. Know and believe it as gospel as it does really work. You won't know, though, until you try it.

I believe that life is a circle. We are just at a point where we are returning to basics trying to understand why and who we are. We are also trying to find out why we do the things the way we do, and maybe why we should have changed the things we did. This is good for all of us and it is also why I believe you will enjoy this book. I also believe the return to basics can help us make a better future.

This book has many of the details I have not been able to find anywhere in any of the protocols published as there are few with the actual details especially that of our gay culture. What I could find for the most part is from the Straight world so its accuracy for our gay culture after reading through it didn't match my memory at all or very little. Here I actually state the words in the ceremonies and truths as I know them to be in my times and life in the "Old Guard" time being knowledgeable of what was done to me and for me and in my behalf. I have also reached out to some of my "Old Guard" friends for their memories and recollection of what we went through. It was interesting to hear some of their stories as well for most of them matched mine.

I recently even got a report from one of my friends who wasn't from the 60's but the late 70's and early 80's and he recalls much of his introduction to the life of leather and it wasn't far from mine, a little more free as life had changed, but he still remembers things like not pursuing a Master/Sir in a bar; that they had to make contact with you not you with them. You would just respond after being summoned to his side, only answering "Yes Sir" or "No Sir" and within a very short time be off to serve him in whatever way he wanted with no negotiations. So we all concluded that life was very different than today and no one has talked about those times in any research I could find.

I would like to add some of his report for your review and enjoyment. "Unlike today, back then it seemed to be the standard that bottoms did not approach a top in a bar. Instead you would allow the top to make eye contact with you. If he was interested, he would motion for you to come over to him and present yourself to him. You were to greet him as follows, "Good Evening Sir. May I be of service?"

"Another difference from today is that there was very limited discussion beyond that. As a bottom, you did not discuss your likes and dislikes – that was inconsequential to the scene; you were there for his pleasure, not yours. In most cases, the top didn't really even speak to you; he would just lead you out of the bar."

"I remember one of the first times I went to a bar after I got out of college. There was a very hot man in full leather standing in a corner smoking a cigar. He motioned for me to approach him and when I was standing in front of him, he exhaled smoke into my face. I replied simply by saying, "Thank you Sir." We left for his playroom right after that."

"Even though it has been a lot of years since I got my training, this is still my primary modus operandi when I'm in a leather bar. Quite often it still works."

"Several years ago, I was out while visiting New York. A man in uniform made eye contact with me, signaling me to approach. When I got close, he pointed towards his Dehners. I dropped to my knees and began licking them. After I had proven myself as a good bootlicker, he took me home, bound me and flogged the crap out of me. I was sore for several days."

I showed this to another friend of mine who is a boy and he said the following "How today would you even be able to do this as many people wear covers including some bottoms. How would you know who is who or what to say to whom?" I returned by saying "exactly right you couldn't and that is why we have lost so much of what was once a vital part of our lives. We used to be able to tell who was who by what they wore and what they wore told us what level would be expected. Today none of that holds true."

My personal experience of people who have learned the "Old Guard" traditions is that they uniformly exhibit both higher degrees of skill and caring for their partners as compared to the degree of lack of skill, caring and control for partners and other people in the community which is so prevalent today.

My last comment before getting to the actual protocols was a question recently asked of me about teaching extreme BDSM and I include this as it truly needs to be carried on in our life! WHY should we teach extreme classes in our lifestyle, you ask? Well if we don't, several things will happen which are not positive. In this time where people are learning things through the internet and through watching videos many of these educational venues don't talk about the techniques or pitfalls behind edge play. People are getting seriously hurt and even dying because of the lack of education in extreme BDSM.

First off, I am a teacher of extreme BDSM and teach everything from blood sports to crucifixion and more including carotid breath play. I have seen others teach simple classes and not be properly educated and cause such things like telling people to use 90 percent isopropyl alcohol instead of 70 percent in fire play. The difference is night and day. My dear friend Lamalani, IMsL 2009, and I were just talking about a class where someone was teaching fire play. The instructor didn't mention using only cotton thread/string to make the fire wand they used nylon thread/string and cause burns on the demo bottom in a fire class. If good teachers are teaching, then extreme BDSM should be taught so everyone can get correct information.

Extreme caution must be met when interviewing an educator at any level. There are good ones in every community, resource them and get them to teach. That goes from basic flogging to advance suspension, or blood sports. If the educator is thoroughly educated in the extreme play then he/she should pass that information on to his fellow leathermen that want to learn it. If not, when the feather tickles the Dom to do it, they may end up seriously hurting someone.

We all grow through this journey doing more extreme play as we grow, I am sure everyone of you would agree that the flogging you do today is much more extreme than when you started, or the whip play or the sounding or whatever it is that flips your button. You got there through education and learning.

Why would you or any organization not want to teach the extreme? Are you afraid of being blamed for teaching something or someone a wrong technique? Well then you shouldn't teach it or practice it. There is extreme to every type of play as well. I have seen an extreme whipping scene much more brutal, savage and edgy then my harp scene, 100 needles inserted and zippered causing extreme blood, as many of you have seen. I don't understand why we would want to limit ourselves as leatherfolk. From the "Old Guard" Days we have learned many things. We have changed them to protect ourselves and our future. We will learn new and better ways, but if we don't give them the foundation to build upon, they will not be able to go into the future. Extreme BDSM is about edge play and too many ask where is the edge? When and where should that edge be determined? I ask you who are you to even ask that question? Isn't it up to the two consenting adults?

One should know the medical side of CPR and other first aid practices to resuscitate the bottom should it become necessary. Extreme BDSM is out there and if we don't protect what we do and teach it to our newer members of the community it will die, we will die. It's like anything else in this life of ours, we must pass it on, it's part of whom and what we are and what we owe to our brothers and sisters. Extreme play will always be out there and will always be pushed farther and farther. It baffles me why a serious leather organization would hinder this education? Not promote it. It's like sex in many ways. We all do it. We all do it differently. So why not learn a new way or make an old way better if you can?

I feel it is part of who and what we are. It's what needs to be done to further everyone's life in our lifestyle. If we don't educate our younger members, they will go on to make horrific mistakes bringing us back to the days of being jailed and hitting the press with bad press of our lifestyle!

"Old Guard" references a time in the BDSM lifestyle when there was much more structure, stability and strictness than there is for the most part today. Anyone interested in exploring the world of Dominance and submission must embrace the concept of structure. Without structure, it is impossible to achieve stability within a Master/Sir/boy/boi/submissive/slave relationship. Without strictness there was no stability. So you can see they all tie back to one another.

Dominance was and is power and authority. The ability to inspire the compliance of others with the Master's/Sir's desires was and is a true talent. Such power and authority was unquestionably part of the "real world" and still is today. There was no reason, culturally, socially or otherwise, why Masters/Sirs and their boy/boi/submissive/slaves would not be able to retain the real essence of their relationship while fully immersed in the real world. I did and still believe this can be done today. Yes it takes work and practice along with routines but it can truly happen producing a wonderful life.

ETTIQUETTE VS PROTOCOL VS RITUAL

Etiquette:

Etiquette represents a set of rules that guide us toward the right way of interacting with others in the world. It is culture bound and situation bound. It represents a way of showing respect to others while demonstrating your understanding of good manners. Manners are the key words. Etiquette can be said to be outward looking, describing the way you interact with others within our culture, external to the Master/slave structure. Emily Post probably was known worldwide as the queen of etiquette.

Protocols:

Protocols represent a new set of rules that govern specific actions or behavior in a particular situation. Protocols however are inward looking. Protocols are actions and behaviors versus manners in etiquette. They describe the way the Master/Sir wishes his boy/boi/submissive/ slave to do specific things within the Master/Sir/boy/boi/submissive/slave structure. How the two interact with each other is Protocol. For example my boy always stands at my right side because I am right hand dominant. Therefore, my natural way to turn to talk to someone is to my right. Within my leather group, protocol represents our way of interacting with each other and others that come to visit us, our common courtesy to one another. Protocols are expressed as a Code of Conduct within our community.

Rituals/Traditions:

Rituals are like traditions. Ways that we choose to do things that are repeated with some regularity, but without a set of rules that govern specific behavior. Much like at New Year's Eve where some people eat herring, or corned beef and cabbage, or even black eyed peas for good luck depending on your heritage. This would be classified a tradition or ritual. Ceremonies are rituals and traditions.

TYPES OF "OLD GUARD" PROTOCOLS

The three types of protocols were established for all leathermen but mainly for collared boy/boi/submissive/slaves and their owners in the community.

There were three levels or types of protocol. They were simple enough to be remembered and applied, yet flexible enough to survive the stress of daily life. Reinforcing these protocols in both the Master/Sir and boy/boi/submissive/slave, no matter what the context, there were applicable rules and standards, providing everyone with a firm ground work within which to relate to each other, in confidence and satisfaction. It provided structure, stability and strictness. Protocol shows the proper respect at the proper time and place.

Most of the time, social or low protocol prevailed. It became second hand for most of us. Master and I had lots of high protocol events. His position in the community made it more demanding for me with more frequent high protocol events. However, even high protocol became second nature for me. I think the key here is, no matter what happens, low protocol is the most common protocol in any situation. As long as everyone remembers that, no one would be offended if you used low protocol in any situation. If I had to state one protocol to commit to memory it would be low protocol.

High protocol gave me the ability to really show off the dedication to service to my Master. He seemed so proud of me when we were in High protocol situations. I would show him that it was him who made me feel incredible. It was so gratifying for both of us when I did display this level of protocol. Again, this protocol is one that isn't used often but, if you have a high profile Master/Sir or even a high profile boy/boi/submissive/slave, both need to know these protocols. They certainly are more demanding and command the ultimate in service and in respect. I also learned that in some situations even though you were in high protocol things could not always be done properly. I would default back to low protocol if I couldn't perform the high protocol to the utmost. I guess what I am saying here is, if you can perform the high protocols in a high protocol situation, it is great for both parties. But if for some reason you can't, use low protocol. i.e. one boy I owned since then could not get down all the time on one knee due to a knee injury. I allowed him to have low protocols for certain positions and high protocol for other situations. He would use a combination of low and high protocol in these high protocol events. This is a very important factor here and needs to be discussed before the boy is trained in high protocol as well as each high protocol situation.

Protocols were created to be inward looking with respect shown. If you can't do it well, you are not honoring anyone. In fact you may be disgracing yourself or your Master/Sir. The boy/boi/submissive/slave may feel humiliated because he can't perform it. So understand it has to be a win win for both parties. Protocols are inward giving and searching. If one can't do it well, they tend not to feel good about themselves doing it. So if you are going to a high protocol event, practice and know your limitations. Only honor those that you can perform well. Eventually, if you are in good health with no limitations, I promise you that you will conquer this protocol as well and find the feeling high protocol can give to both the Master/Sir and the boy/boi/submissive/slave.

Social Protocol

Usually used when not in a Leather establishment or event. What would be a non-leather establishment? E.g. a grocery store, any retail establishment other than leather store, malls, work environment, airport, non-leather social events, non-leather parties, any place where people are gathered and they are not wearing leather.

- The boy was to refer to a Master/Sir as "Sir" and by His given name only if Sir seems inappropriate for some reason. There were no other language restrictions.

- The Master/Sir would not call the boy with his title just his stated name ie: John, James etc.

- The boy was free to speak or ask questions without limitation of anyone.

- The boy/boi/submissive/slave may walk almost next to Master/Sir and in all other ways appear like a vanilla couple. In a group setting, the boy was released from having to maintain eye contact at all times.

- Rituals still applied. Namely, getting Master/Sir a drink or food, or attending to his needs socially. A boy would always request permission to go to the bathroom or any place out of the sight of the Sir. This question sometime could be done as follows: " Sir I am going to the restroom if you need me" or "John, I am going to the restroom if you need me". The Master/Sir may just nod as confirmation to the statement. This would cause less concern in public than the literal asking for permission in a vanilla environment, then awaiting verbal confirmation.

- A boy/boi/submissive/slave's collar should be hidden and not be obvious in public display. It can be worn under a shirt or jacket and tie for example. The collar would never come off unless the boy/boi/submissive/slave's life was in jeopardy.

- The boy/slave/submissive may serve his Master/Sir as a waiter, minimizing point position. He would not serve from a kneeling position.

- Social Protocol would be used when in the presence of vanilla observers. During that time of social protocol, no one should be obvious in any position or title. However, in introductions the Master's name would be introduced first then the Sir's and then the boy/boi/submissive/slave's real names without title. i.e. James, John, Bill, mike, tom, steve. (I used caps and lowercase just to show somewhat their title without revealing their title.)

- The boy/slave/submissive would not kneel unless ordered to do so. The boy/boi/submissive/slave may sit on the floor, if it would not draw attention. If the boy/slave/submissive uses furniture, he would do so by sitting as close to his Master/Sir as possible, making his body accessible to his Master/Sir as much as possible, without being obvious.

- Overall social protocol was the dropping of many things but still maintained discipline following as much protocol as could be done without causing suspicion or any other issues for any one. This is really the bottom line in Social protocol!

- Boy would always have a cutter and lighter for the Master/Sir's cigars and or cigarettes. He would still light his Master/Sir's first should the occasion occur. Otherwise always be ready to light anyone else's cigar or cigarette should the Master/Sir not be smoking.

Low Protocol

Usually used when at a Leather establishment, a leather bar, or any leather social where high protocol would not be appropriate. Low protocols would be used whenever it would not be looked down at, such as a leatherman's home or private social function. Walking and standing protocols were invoked plus the following.

- The boy/slave/submissive was to refer to his Master/Sir as "Sir", and by His given name, e.g. Sir John. Just Sir seemed inappropriate, for some reason in low protocol. Since he was among other leatherfolk or in a leather friendly environment, the respect he had achieved should be shown. Same would apply for the boy/boi/submissive/slave. e.g. slave george, boy sean. All titles would be used with their names.

- The boy/slave/submissive would not kneel unless ordered to do so, but would sit on the floor. If the boy/slave/submissive was allowed to use furniture, he would do so by sitting as close to his Master/Sir as possible. He would make his body accessible to his Master/Sir as much as possible. The sitting on the furniture would only be done once approval was received from his Master/Sir.

- The boy/slave/submissive would serve his Master/Sir as a waiter might. This includes food and beverage. However, he would serve in standing present position rather than from a kneeling position while he was in public. He would never present service in an on point position. The rules still would apply to serve from the left and remove from the right. Beverages were always served

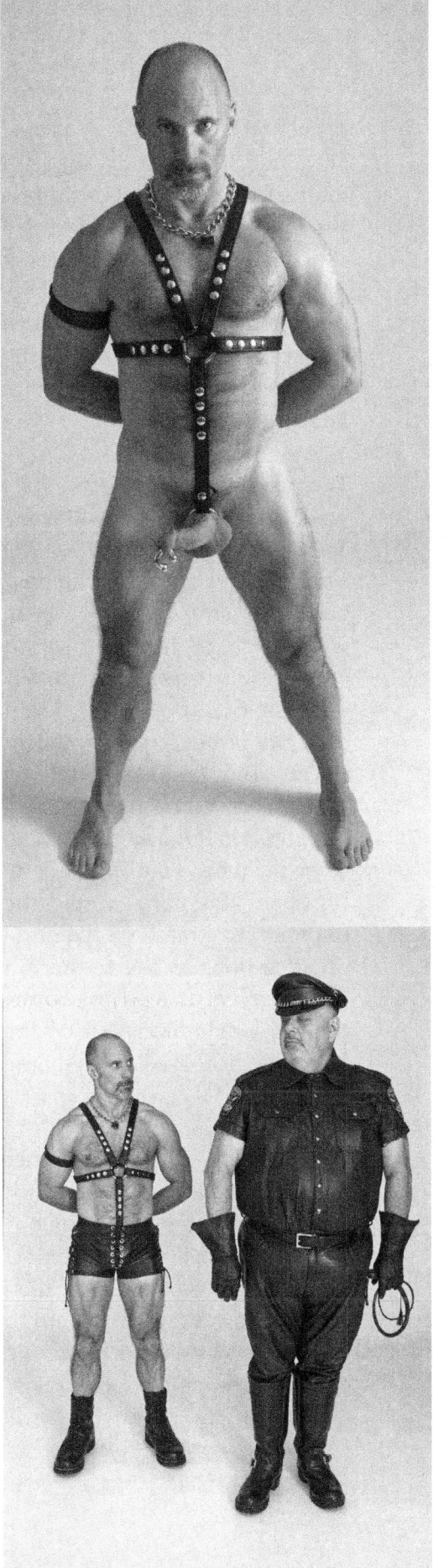

with the boys' right hand extended serving to the Master/Sir.

- Once a boy would enter his Master/Sir's home he would be required to strip down and stand on point to await the Master/Sir's first order and directions if they were alone. Depending on the Master/Sir's home protocol, he may or may not strip if other leathermen were present. This would have been discussed prior to the guests arriving. Proper low protocol would be for the boy to ask the owner of the home if he would like to have the boys naked, as a sign of respect amongst leather folk, if he was visiting without his Master/Sir, to another Master/Sir's home. If he was visiting with his Master/Sir, the Master/Sir should do the asking, if he is unsure of the household rules.

- A boy, once engaged in conversation with a Master/Sir, would simply not wander off. If the Master/Sir was not interested or owned him, the boy would be dismissed. At that point, the boy if not owned would be able to wander off. It was disrespectful to disengage with a Master/Sir if he showed interest even if the boy/boi/submissive/slave was not interested. If the boy/boi/submissive/slave was with his Master/Sir, he would move when his Master/Sir would move, showing service to his Master/Sir.

- If a boy became not interested in the Master/Sir, the boy would ask politely "Master/Sir may I be

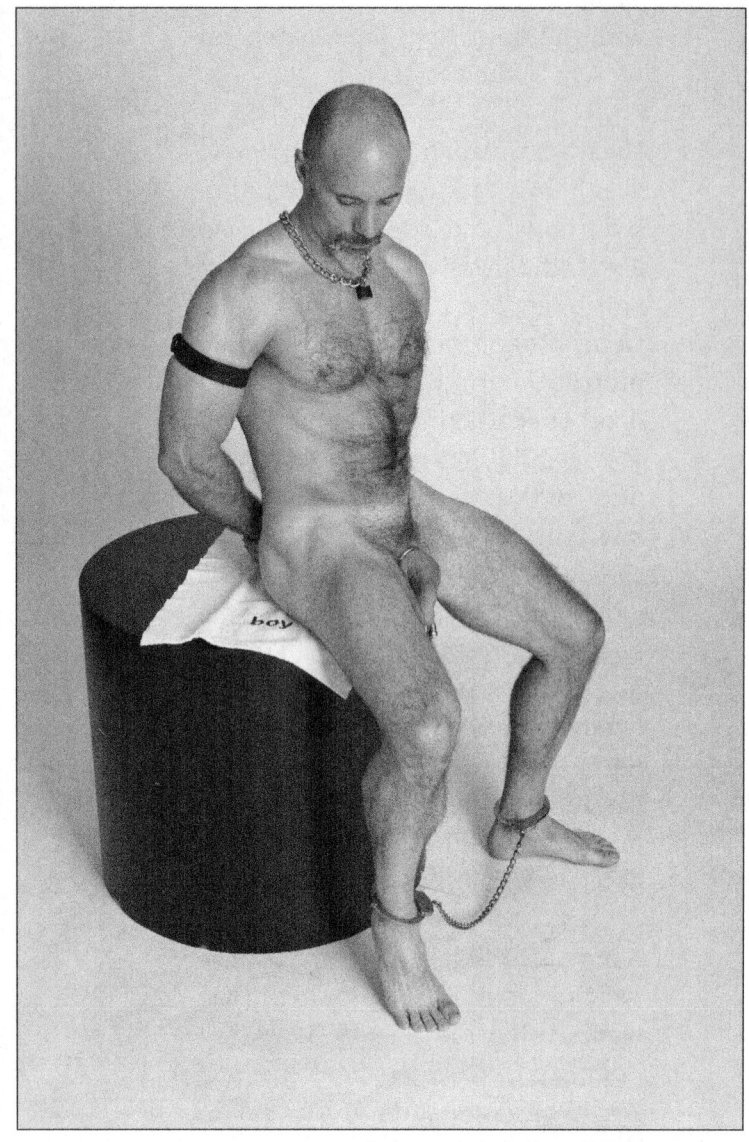

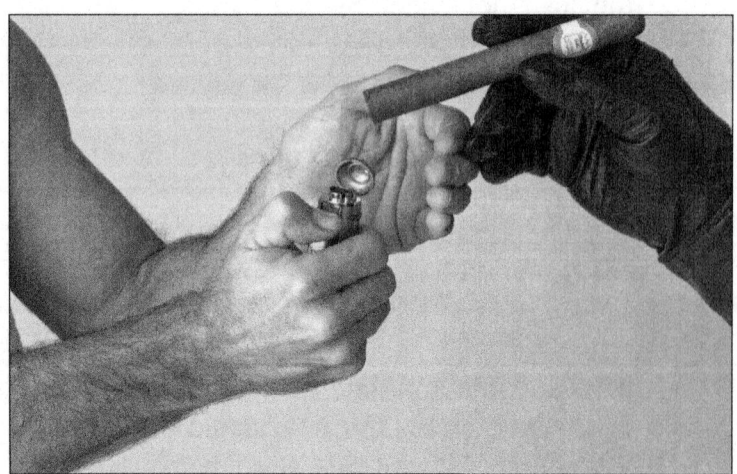

dismissed?" If the Master/Sir understood and was not interested, he would then dismiss the boy to freely move about if he was not collared. If he wasn't dismissed, the boy would stay until he was dismissed, somehow trying to show through the questions and his answers that he was not interested.

- The owned or collared boy would not sit until the Master/Sir had been seated. When the Master/Sir was seated, the boy/boi/submissive/slave's head would not be higher than his Master/Sir's unless it was totally impossible due to the height of the boy/boi/submissive/slave. The boy would remain in eye contact with his Master/Sir and would ask permission to go anywhere out of eyesight. However, the boy would be required to stand on point in public as long as the Master/Sir was standing. In a private home, the boy would always sit on the floor unless otherwise negotiated or stipulated.

- A boy would always have a cutter and lighter for the Master/Sir's cigars and or cigarettes. The boy would always light his Master/Sir's cigar or cigarette first then proceed to others. It was up to the Master/Sir as to whether he cut and prepped his own cigar and the cigars of his guests. In high protocol the boy would always do the cutting as well as the lighting.

- A boy was allowed to engage in conversation with other boys, submissives and slaves but would refrain from starting any conversation's with any Master/Sir. The boy was able to speak without restrictions from boy to boy/boi/submissive/slave. However, for the purposes of reaffirmation and focus of who they are, they were always to use their titles when addressing one another. For example "boy travis would like to know what boy john is thinking" or "boy john is honoring Sir Steven with being available 24/7 for his needs, don't you boy mark want to offer your services 24/7 to Sir Jason?" It was not proper or encouraged just for a boy to use his first name only in low protocol. If it was one boy speaking to someone with another title he would use it as well e.g: "boy john would like to know what slave george is thinking?"

- The boy would be prepared to open all doors or resolve any issues with stairs/doorways/car doors. He would remain and close all doors for his Master/Sir, then do guests and finally his own doors. In "Old Guard" Protocol the Master/Sir's hands were usually gloved and his gloves should remain untouched by things like brass polish and other things which were not leather. This would also keep the gloves sanitary for use in breath control and other types of play near the face, which possibly could cause an infection on a face of a boy. When it comes to stairways a boy would always look for alternate ways to avoid the Master/Sir from touching the railing. He would offer his arm or shoulder for the Master/Sir's stability for the same reason of the glove being sanitary as well as the hands should they not be gloved. I am trying to help you understand that a Master/Sir's hands or gloves were always to remain clean from things that might contaminate the gloves or hands for sanitary reasons. Obviously car doors also fall under this section as well. The boy would always open the Master/Sir's door first, then that of the guests with his being the last to enter the vehicle. He would assist all people in the car from the Master/Sir to the guests. This of course was if the boy was not going to be squeezed in the middle of two other people in a car or vehicle.

Low Protocols were in place wherever and whenever possible.

Low protocols would be used as the basic protocols when not told as to what protocol was to be used. These protocols should be acted on with as much discretion as possible.

HIGH PROTOCOL
FORMAL – HIGH COW – or at all Leather events

ALWAYS used when at a formal leather function, event, seminar, etc. This is looked upon as the high society of Leather Protocol.

All formal protocols were invoked – most especially, the language and attending protocols. The boy/boi/submissive/slave's sole purpose was to serve his Master/Sir and to make Master/Sir's life easier.

- The boy was not to engage in discourse and certainly not to speak unless spoken to. This is a very critical protocol under high protocol as a boy was to be available for his Master/Sir but not open to comment; but he could make notes and be available to serve his Master/Sir only. A boy could of course speak if he was spoken to by a Master/Sir but only, answer the question at hand then return to silence. Of course it would always begin with "Master/Sir this boy would say", and "thank you Master/Sir for asking this boy for his opinion". Or whatever words would appropriately end the sentence.

- The boy was expected to remain highly alert to any logistical issue or problem that may need to be solved. Boy would be expected to remind his Master/Sir of someone's name or taking a business card being offered to Master/Sir from another person. Here is a real service to a Master like me. I am good with faces but terrible with names. I have met so many people through the journey of my life as a Master, I remember faces, but never can remember names. I always ask my boy to bone up on the local people if he can by face and name from previous cards. This way he can assist me and help me with the names. He does this also when we return from a city. He will file the cards by city and make any necessary notes on the back of their respective card. This is done so when we go back to that city, he has an easier access to the local people, rather than random search through my cards trying to find out who is in the city I'm visiting. It is very important, especially with cards, for a Master/Sir not to be out of his cards for future references and meetings/invitations etc. The boy should graciously accept the card from any Master/Sir on behalf of his Master/Sir and make any notes on the back of the card regarding the meeting. This is for future use for his Master/Sir. With these notes the Master/Sir can have some reference as to how they met the person or what was important in that discussion. He would also present the card of his Master/Sir to the guest/Master/Sir in proper form. This is done with both hands, using his finger tips of the fore finger and the thumb. Holding the tips of the top of the card outward. Presenting it so the receiving Master/Sir can read the card easily. This is truly an "Old Guard" tradition of presentation and represents years of protocols and proper introduction. This is a major custom not only amongst leathermen but worldwide in different cultures.

- The boy would remain **ON POINT** at all times shadowing his Master/Sir's every move. **On point** means the following position (parade rest) slightly behind the Master/Sir's right shoulder. (if right hand dominant)

The boy's head bowed slightly, but with full vision of his Master/Sir. So long as Sir was standing, the boy would remain standing in that physical location. If Master/Sir wished to come around to a position facing him, he would either instruct the boy to move into his range of vision or used the family's silent hand signals to cause the boy to change positions. The boy's hands would be behind his back with his left hand clutching his right, just above the wrist, unless otherwise engaged to perform a duty.

- The boy would be prepared to open all doors or resolve any issues with stairs/doorways/car doors. He would remain and close all doors for his Master/Sir, then do guests and finally his own doors. This would be the same as in low protocol.

- A boy should always acknowledge with a quick head bowing to acknowledge the hand signals if used and given. This gives the recognition back to the Master/Sir that the boy has received the hand signal and will obey as quickly as possible maintaining silence.

- Everyone would use all titles in conversation. e.g. Master John would like to meet Sir James and boy jeff. Have slave george attend to their drinks.

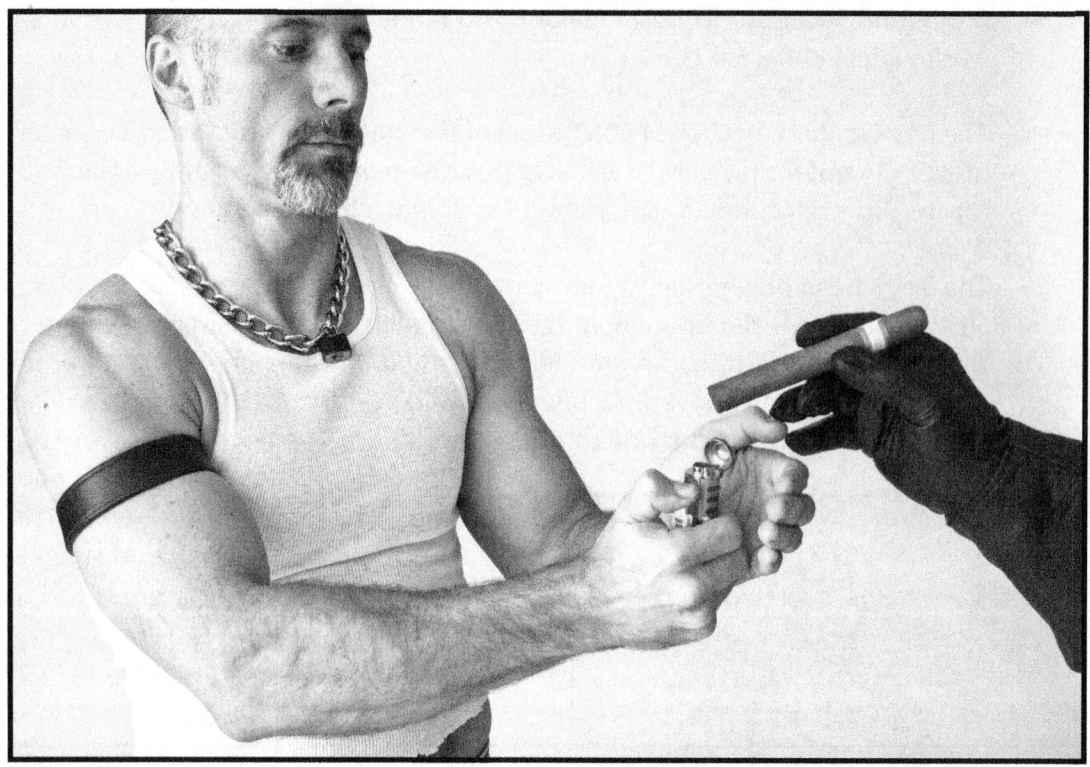

- The boy would always have a cigar cutter and lighter for the Master/Sir's cigars or cigarettes. In high protocol he would always do the cutting and lighting of his Master/Sir's cigar/cigarette first, and then do the same for the other Masters/Sirs/guests. In high protocol situations many Master/Sirs enjoy cigars as a way to relax and talk amongst other Master/Sirs. Cigars have always been very critical in "Old Guard" as they had a reference to power and real strong players, along with gloves. Obviously in high protocol situations, cigar play would not be an acceptable way to dispose of any ash or any other type of play as high protocol was just that. Cigar play would be kept for lower protocol situations as well as for private and dungeon scenes.

- The boy would never wear gloves of any sort. Gloves were meant for the Master/Sirs only and a boy was not to touch the Master/Sir's gloves unless told to do so by his Master/Sir. Gloves are a sign of hard play BDSM. Gloves are very common in both low and high protocol attire for a Master/Sir. Gloves should never leave the Master/Sir's body. If he wasn't going to be wearing them, they should be kept on his body in a pocket displaying some part of the glove or through an epaulette on his shirt or some other place where they still can be seen, such as being clasped in his hands. They would never be worn in social protocol.

- The boy would always hold any object for his Master/Sir during conversation, e.g. his jacket/cover etc. or any other types of objects, pamphlets, invitations even his drink if the Master/Sir was wearing gloves. As far as anything else would go, the boy would be responsible for either holding it or taking it to the proper area e.g. a cloak room for his jacket and cover. Under high protocol situations the boy would be in constant attention of his Master/Sir. The boy/boi/submissive/slave would always be showing the highest level in service yet remaining silent. In high protocol the Master's/Sir's gloves need to remain with the Master/Sir. If needed, the boy needs to ensure the gloves remain with his Master/Sir. Should the gloves be left in any garment, the boy would be sure to give the Master/Sir gloves to him. He then would take whatever garment to the place designated by the Master/Sir.

- The boy would always have a fresh drink or beverage for his Master/Sir and always anticipate the finishing of the drink. When this would happen, the boy needed to get him a new one without even a question being asked. Here, there was hopefully some familiarity with the boy. If the boy was in service for just that evening and hadn't gotten to be familiar with his Master/Sir for the night, obviously he would need to find out prior to his Master/Sir engaging in any conversation how and what he would want to drink. He would also need to find out how he would want to be attended to. However, if a boy had been in service to a Master/Sir for a while and was familiar with his drinking habits and types of drinks, the boy would always be sure it was done according to that Master's/Sir's wishes. The Master/Sir may have given him money to pay for the drinks or beverages or if it was at a party where they were supplied, he would check out the availability prior to the Master/Sir engaging in conversation and find out the order of drinks or what type of drinks he would accept during the party. It was up to the boy to maintain a beverage for his Master/Sir for the rest of the evening. Should the boy run out of money prior to the evening from the Master/Sir, the boy would continue the drinks and expect to be paid back if the Master/Sir was only his for the evening. If he was a collared boy that would have to be negotiated depending if the Master/Sir maintained the control of the boy's expense money. Again, it is never assumed that the Master/Sir's drinks are paid for by the boy/boi/submissive/slave. A Master/Sir should always be sure the boy is not being put in a position to have to pay for the Master/Sir's drinks out of his own money unless this has been negotiated.

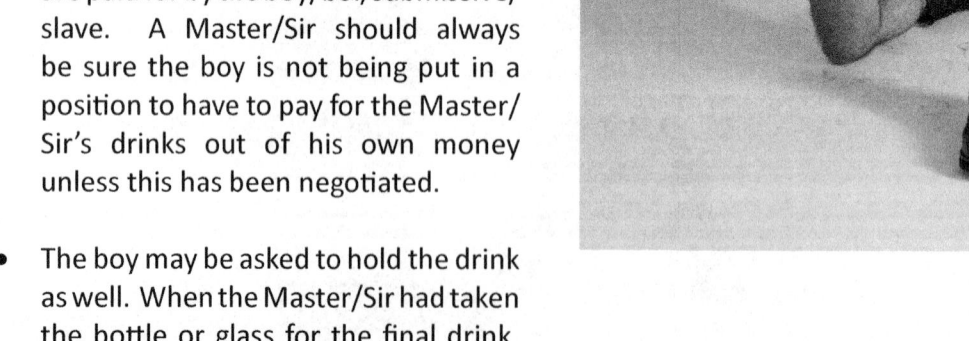

- The boy may be asked to hold the drink as well. When the Master/Sir had taken the bottle or glass for the final drink, he would silently disappear with a nod of his head acknowledging the Masters/Sirs with respect and slip off and return with the new drink. Here again, a boy needed to know how his Master/Sir wanted to have the drinks presented or held. When I was in service, this was the way my Master always wanted me: on my knees, at his side, holding the glass upward for his easy reach.

Many Masters/Sirs did not do this even back then, but it was "Old Guard" protocol. This protocol however makes it obvious that I was truly his boy, presenting his drink constantly in this fashion. For all you boy/submissive/slaves, trust me, it wasn't easy to hold this position for long. I had to always watch for my Masters hand to drop. I soon learned that when Master's hand dropped, he would want his drink presented for him to just pick up out of my hand. Be sure if you are going to follow this protocol, understand your arms might get sore from holding the drink in the air. Negotiate how he wants you to hold his drink. Negotiate how this is to be done as well as his drink selections from the Master/Sir you're in service to. You can also hold it close to your body or in your lap presenting upward when the Master/Sir drops his hand. The boy, with the drop of the Master/Sirs hand, extends his hand upward or outward, holding the drink for his acceptance of that drink. This is a much easier pose to maintain for long periods. This would also be proper High Protocol. You may also rest on your haunches instead of being on your knees if you were going to be there for a long period. Being on one knee servicing in this manner is very hard unless you just drop to your knee to present, then re-stand after the Master/Sir has taken his drink. This can be a very effective way to serve many drinks to many Masters/Sirs as well. Again be sure you service your Master/Sir first if this should occur. A boy/boi/submissive/slave would always attend to his Master/Sir first prior to attending to any other Master/Sir.

- Whenever the Master/Sir moved about and ended a conversation with another Master/Sir, the boy/boi/submissive/slave would always stand on point position and bow his head acknowledging the other Master/Sir with his end of participation in the conversation. This was done prior to moving on with his Master/Sir, whether or not he was invited into the conversation. It just showed the other Master/Sir respect for his position and that the boy acknowledged that position.

- Whenever possible, if the boy/boi/submissive/slave is the only one other than the Masters/Sirs in the conversation, he should try to serve all the Masters/Sirs as best he can but always remembering his Masters/Sirs would come first. He would of course remain silent unless spoken to and continue serving, always serving all the Masters first prior to the Sirs. If it is totally impossible to do this and maintain proper high protocol to your Master/Sir then don't do anything for anyone other than your Master/Sir and explain that you are sorry you are not able to serve the other Masters/Sirs due to the number of them or whatever the reason may be. You may apologize to the other Masters/Sirs stating "I can only be in service to my Master/Sir tonight."

High protocol is very difficult for a boy/boi/submissive/slave. It requires much more attention to the Master/Sir. If you are going to learn this protocol, know that if you're the Master/Sir it is much more exhausting for the boy/boi/submissive/slave and take into consideration what the boy/boi/submissive/slave is doing and be aware of his exhaustion. You as the Master/Sir need to show the respect back to his position, with thank you's and other considerations. Master would sometimes see me tiring. He would then move about not talking to anyone but me. This would give me the time to move my joints, relax my muscles and get the circulation moving in my legs and arms. Remember in high protocol, the Master/Sir and boy/boi/submissive/slave need to work as a team and be respectful of their relationship. Be sure that the respect and trust go both ways. The boy/boi/submissive/slave needs to know his strengths and stability and understand how strict the Master/Sir wants to uphold this high protocol. I also recommend maybe having two sets of High protocols so that the Master/Sir can make a ruling. If the High protocol will be for a short period, he can expect the highest protocols. If it is going to be an extended period of high protocols, he may allow some relaxed protocols. Again, all this is up for negotiation, but these were the standards set forth along with some personal modifications due to my experience as a boy. Personally, I used to love the high protocol times, as it allowed me to shine as a boy. I was so proud of my Master and being in service to him. High protocols allowed me so much pride to serve him like this. He would glow being proud as people would ask him as to how I was trained. He use to laugh, and say well he is like this all the time. I just didn't know what to do with him. So I let him do as he liked. That's when I knew he was gloating over my service and I would step it up again. I would come home from some high protocol events and almost collapse. I was so exhausted. boys/bois/submissives/ slaves prepare yourself for these events. Rest and allow yourself the opportunity to shine for your Master/Sir!

"OLD GUARD" RULES AND PROTOCOLS

A well-implemented protocol is uniquely useful in providing guidance and structure even during times that are casual and relaxed. Very importantly, they allow a boy/boi/submissive/slave to have a secure understanding of what is expected of him in different contexts, in different circumstances of formality and informality. The Master/Sir would simply specify to the boy/boi/submissive/slave "This evening boy will be spent in low protocol", and all parties then would know exactly what would be the expectations and standards which would be applied to everyone's interactions that evening.

Ideally, a tiered system of protocol levels are simple enough to be remembered and applied, yet flexible enough to survive the stress of daily life, reinforcing in both the Master/Sir and the boy/boi/submissive/slave that, no matter what the context, there are applicable rules and standards, providing everyone with a firm groundwork within which to relate to each other as a Master/Sir and a boy/boi/submissive/slave, in confidence and satisfaction to all parties involved.

In "Old Guard" settings:

- Protocol for boys/bois/ submissives/slaves traditionally meant wearing black or preferably white t-shirts/tank tops known as wife beaters, blue or black jeans or leather shorts, white socks if any, black boots (laced right over left denoting a boy/boi/submissive/slave) or other black shoes.

    Today colors are in fashion and colored socks and colored t-shirts are acceptable amongst many levels denoting one's likes and fetishes in the leather lifestyle. However, white t shirt/tank top and blue jeans would be "Old Guard" traditional wear.

- Protocol was and still is not intended to give every Master/Sir the permission to top or dominate every boy/ boi/ submissive/slave. This was and still is an important protocol. Even in today's leather life, many people think that they

can just do what they want with any boy/ boi/ submissive/slave. This is not true. When I meet people like this it greatly annoys me. I always tend to ask who gave them permission to do what they are doing to that boy/boi/submissive/slave. It is always fun to see what they respond and say. I hear a lot "well I'm a Dom Top I can do whatever I want". I generally say back to them "Oh Really! Who died and left you in charge of everyone?"

- Protocol does not define the relationship between a Master/Sir and a boy/boi/submissive/slave nor does it define it just between a Master/Sir and a boy/boi/submissive/slave.

- Protocol was and still is for all leatherfolk, regardless of title or rank.

- Protocol does not define the relationship between friends; that is etiquette.

- Protocol was not and still is not a way for a Master/Sir to feel superior over another person. It doesn't define the boy/boi/submissive/slave's way to feel subservient.

- Protocol was and is not a rigid adherence to rules or traditions.

- Protocol was and is not a way to define how people play.

- Protocol was and still is a code of conduct and mostly it is the basic manners that were taught you by your mother.

- Never touch another leatherman's cover (motorcycle cap or head gear) unless you were very intimate friends or lovers or in service to them. When touched, never touch the patent leather brim! The cover was always removed by the sides when removing it. When a submissive carried the cover it was always carried with the cover upright never upside down.

When a Master/Sir kept it other than on his head it would be kept under his left arm with the open part of the cover to his body, brim pointing forward. In that manner the cover was protected and wrapped the body to help keep the shape of the cover.

- A Master/Sir's words were golden. Promises was always kept. boy/boi/submissive/ slaves were always not to challenge any request by the Master/Sir at any time. They could however, if unclear, ask questions so they would be in the position to properly execute the order or request given.

- In the home, a boy/boi/submissive/slave(s), were to remain naked and collared at all times. slaves would possibly be in shackles.

He would remain on his knees awaiting an order if he was not doing a previous order, with his hands behind his back, left grasping the right hand and his head slightly bowed showing respect with enough eye contact to acknowledge his Master/Sir and any order forth coming. He then would rise and proceed with the order given, proceed naked with his hands behind his back until such time he needed them for completing the order given. During rest times at home the boy would always sit on the floor unless otherwise negotiated with the Master/Sir and at the Master's/Sir's feet. The boy could relax at this point and enjoy the relaxed time with his Master/Sir. During relaxed time at home the boy can speak freely with his Master/Sir as in normal conversation but always using Sir to address his Master/Sir.

Circumstances may occur which would be dictated by the Master/Sir where clothing was necessary, such as when non leather guests were expected at the Master/Sir's home who were not aware of the lifestyle. This typically was repairmen, service type people or parents and friends who were not in the lifestyle. The Master/Sir then would approve the boy/boi/submissive/slave attire depending on who was arriving. In some households, there was a uniform of sorts that was used. This was not done so that the boy would learn humility, degradation or sexual gratification. It was done to have the boy practice obedience and discipline and to remove all earthly values so he could practice and focus on his service to his Master. If there were some circumstances, i.e. a handicap or some other special consideration that needed to be dealt with, this sometimes varied.

- boy/boi/submissive/slave would always carry a butt towel when naked to prevent any stains on the floor, carpet or other places. Obviously a boy/boi/submissive/slave butt should always be clean, but if the boy just had sex or some other type of play and was told to hold whatever and maintain whatever was inside of him, he could have an accident and this towel was used to prevent any accidents. Let's face it boys, we can try to always be clean, but it doesn't always happen, therefore use the butt towel to prevent any issues.

- A boy's/boi's/submissive's/slave's demeanor would always be humble and respectful yet not robotic. The boy/boi/submissive/slave would strive to maintain a pleasant attitude, as would the Master/Sir, during the course of their day no matter what the duty. It was a customary saying a happy Master/Sir meant the boy/boi/submissive/slave was happy. Never would a boy show any signs of disrespect in service. If a boy/boi/submissive/slave was unhappy he would still approach his Master/Sir in a happy way and ask for permission for a private conversation. Then when given the audience with the Master/Sir, he would then be allowed to open up and speak freely. If not, the boy/boi/submissive/

slave would always maintain the happy demeanor.

- First time each day, the boy/boi/submissive/slave would see their or any Master/Sir, they would stand at **Point Position** and present themselves as to greet them good morning. If the Master/Sir smiled at his slave, the slave could smile back, acknowledging the approval of his Master/Sir. The only words spoken would be thank you Master/SiR.

- A boy/boi/submissive/slave was always at the feet of his Master/Sir when seated therefore furniture was never used for the boy/boi/submissive/slave. A Master/Sir could give a boy permission to use the furniture and maintain that permission providing the Master/Sir approved, but it was customary if the boy/boi/submissive/slave was going out even if permission had been given by his Master/Sir for their home, the boy/boi/submissive/slave would return to the floor when at another Master/Sir's home or anywhere public unless the owner of the home or property gave instructions differently. He also would do what was customary at the other Master's/Sir's home whether or not the boy was to be naked or dressed. Usually this was discussed with his Master/Sir prior to arriving at the other Master/Sir's home so the boy/boi/submissive/slave would know what was expected of him upon arrival. A good Master/Sir would always check on this protocol prior to arriving at the visited home so that he would be able to inform his boy/boi/submissive/slave to avoid both their embarrassments.

- At all times a boy/boi/submissive/slave always had to ask permission to use the restroom. When using the restroom a boy/boi/submissive/slave would always sit never stand. In "Old Guard" ways they were not allowed to use the toilet seat. They were not to close the door. This was done for many reasons. It was felt that a Master/Sir not only could see and hear what the boy/boi/submissive/slave was doing but so that he could also see if the boy/boi/submissive/slave had any issues such as lots of gas or diarrhea. The door was only closed when guests were present. When using the restroom the door was always to remain open otherwise.

- At mealtimes, a boy/boi/submissive/slave would serve the Master's/Sir's meal and would eat after the Master/Sir was finished. In my home today, my boy/boi/submissive/slave will serve me first then sit with me, to my right, at the table. He must attend to my needs during the meal e.g. if my glass was to become empty, he must stop his meal and fill my glass etc. My boy needs to clear my plate and silverware immediately upon my finishing eating and serve my next course should there be one, even if he has not finished his same course. He would be allowed to finish all courses at his own speed however. I will eat all courses at my speed and he must maintain service during my meal. It was also known that in "Old Guard" ways the boy/boi/submissive and slave would eat sitting on the floor. There were also some who felt their boy/boi/submissive/slave should eat after them. Today typically with puppies they eat on the floor and with dog dishes. Master and I always ate together, as we enjoyed the company, but again this is a rule that could be negotiated.

- In serving a Master/Sir whatever he was serving was done on bended knee presenting the item to his Master/Sir in a proper **Formal Half Present** presentation.

- When speaking to a Master/Sir "Old Guard" protocol stated that every sentence would start with the word Master/Sir and end the sentence again with the word Master/Sir. For Example: Master/Sir would you like a beverage Master/Sir? Or if the boy/boi/submissive or slave would ask for himself he must state his title in the sentence ie: Master/Sir, the boy/boi/submissive/slave requests permission to use the bathroom Master/Sir? Today in my house I only ask for one either at the front or back of the sentence. I find that stating Master/Sir at both ends is kind of ridiculous but again this can be negotiated and is my opinion.

- Never use a Master/Sir's first name only unless in social protocol. Always state Master/Sir and then his name, i.e. Master John.

- Profanity was never allowed by a boy/boi/submissive/slave or a Master/Sir. "Old Guard" never used profanity at any time. Again remember the military and respect.

- A boy/boi/submissive/slave was to be clean inside and out, to always be prepared. This was a rule that generally was upheld in every household. Today, this should still be upheld in every Master/Sir-boy/boi/submissive/slave relationship. A boy/boi/submissive/slave would not be used if they were found to be unclean or dirty.

- If boys/bois/submissive/slaves are talking amongst themselves their titles need to be used. No Master/Sir would ever be discussed amongst just the boys/bois/submissives and slaves under any circumstances. For example boy tom would speak to slave michael as follows: "slave michael would you get your brother boy tom the keys to the car?" This was only violated in social protocol which then would state "Michael would you get your brother tom the keys to the car?"

- When in general public areas a Master/Sir and boy/boi/submissive/slave would not try and draw attention to their relationship. However the boy/boi/submissive/slave should try and follow protocol as much as possible without doing so.

- If a boy/boi/submissive/slave were to have a drink while standing, they were never to keep the drink behind their bodies. It was always to be in front of them so the Master/Sir could see what and when they were drinking.

- Do not borrow or lend money. Borrowed money or lending money to a fellow club member always seemed to have issues, causing other issues, not only for the two men involved but usually the issues went over into club business.

- Conduct affairs with honor and integrity.

- Never lie. Our word was known as our bond. If a lie was to happen one would never be able to trust that person again. Trust being one of the keys to our community.

- Never wear another man's leather. If it is gifted down or transferred ownership then it was fine. There are some times in newer times when people are allowed to wear someone else's leather. That is when it is put on by the owner for a purpose as a special event or function or for a particular reason.

- Shower frequently and be deodorant and cologne free. The preference of a natural body scent or a hot sweaty man in leathers is a sexual stimulant and aphrodisiac. Bad body odor is not something that is tolerated. That is why we say shower frequently but you can have your manly smell, not stale old body odor smell. There are however men who love that body odor smell. So, to each his own.

- Never mix brown leather with black leather. It is classified a huge disrespect to each of the leathers to wear one with the other. Brown leather was our first "Old Guard" leather and should never be mixed with the black leather which is also from "Old Guard" time. Brown leather was just what we all started on back in those days as it was more readily available. We would have to dye it then before it could be bought or used as black leather as we do now, whether in skins or hides. Now we almost always buy black leather as died finished skins or hides to make what we need. Black leather now is the universal color leather represented all over the world. In fact, I have worn some old brown leathers and people didn't even recognize me as part of the leather tribe. Please be respectful of those old brown leathermen. Their leathers are generally true "Old Guard". I am finding a resurgence of the brown leathers in leatherwear today.

- Never mix chrome/silver trim with gold/brass trim. Chrome/Silver is classified the highest form of mixture with black leather as the gold/brass was used more frequently on brown leathers.

- Keep studs and other decorations to a tasteful minimum; never wear any types of jewels or rhinestones as it was known to be inappropriate and too queeny/nellie/feminine.

- Leathermen never wear tennis shoes, sandals or dress shoes with leather anything. This is still true; even in Florida where we do wear all of these items, we don't wear them with our leathers.

- Boots were a requirement when in leather. Always black in color if you were wearing black leather. Brown boots would be worn in you were wearing brown leathers. They were to be polished; scuffed boots were never acceptable. Oil tanned boots would be clean and never dirty.

- If you are cruising seriously, wear the keys out; if you are not cruising, tuck them in a back pocket not showing any part of the keys.

- Always indicate strictly leather sex or 'rough sex' interest by wearing keys appropriately.

- Always wear white socks. Masters/Sirs were never allowed to pull their socks up beyond the top of their boot, nor have it substantially above their boot top. Today colored socks are worn to accent the outfit or to flag a color that the person likes as part of his fetish see hanky codes.

- Leathermen never flag on both right and left sides. Flag only one side or the other. If you wanted to switch for the night or week go out of town and do so. In "Old Guard" there was no such thing as a versatile man. We looked at it as if you were clueless as to who you really were. Today versatile men turn many of us "Old Guard" men off as we don't know what you want tonight. As a total top I don't want another top. So to all of you men flagging versatile, you may want to rethink your strategy. Yes we know you think it's the best of both worlds but when cruising it confuses many of us so we tend not to pick you up as we don't know what you want.

- Never wear underwear. If something must be worn under jeans or shorts, wear a jock, athletic or leather or even a cod piece.

- Experience in the Scene determines social seniority Masters then Sirs, Daddies, Tops then boy/boi/submissive and finally slave. Not age, not size, nor amount of leather worn. Definitely not offices held in organizations, awards received or titles won. The only time awards would be recognized are at contests where contest titles have meaning.

- Hair must be worn in a military cut or shaved clean. Hair would always be considered military acceptable. Something else could only be worn if medically necessary.

Today there are many more fashionable haircuts that are acceptable that wouldn't have been military acceptable. Prime would be a Mohawk or other tribal cut.

- Shorts were never worn in formal settings for dominants; boys could wear them, but they would be leather and never cutoff jeans. Cutoff jeans were never worn as shorts by "Old Guard" leathermen as it represented a very untidy look which "Old Guard" Leathermen didn't accept. It wasn't until the 70's when this began to loosen up and was accepted as was the torn jean look but still to this date, for "Old Guard" men wearing leather, it still isn't accepted. Worn look jeans were accepted as it tended to accent our bulges but never torn. Lace up boots would only be worn with shorts as it was the only type of boot that really accented the look of short-wearing boot men. It showed off our muscular legs and hairiness with still the look of a leatherman. In "Old Guard" times torn jeans were only worn by pigs and pigs were not really looked at as we look at them today. In those days, pigs were looked upon as whore types, not respectable men. Now pigs are guys just out after some hot fun times. Remember, the times were very different then.

- Jeans would either be black or blue when worn with chaps. In "Old Guard" days black jeans were not so readily accessible.

- Chaps would be worn bare-assed or with jeans (see above). Chaps would be fitted correctly and never baggy or loose fitted.

    o Chaps indicate a higher level of commitment to leather than jeans and leather pants indicate even higher commitment than chaps. The standard was tight 501 jeans showing the bulge of your crotch encased by the chaps. If black were worn it was always at night as blue jeans were our daily wear.

- Leather belt was required; "Old Guard" only wore basic black with no design, today the basket weave or other design is acceptable as long as nothing fancy or sparkly is added to the belt. Under no circumstances should rhinestones or gems be used to adorn a belt as "Old Guard" was never about flashy. "Old Guard" leathermen always used black black black everything. It wasn't until the 90's really when leather started to be adorned with lots of colors and other things. It was always "Old Guard" tradition for high cow to always be black black black everything. Only adornments were of silver color and maybe brass color. But never could the adornments be mixed. It was always all silver or all brass such as the belt buckles and buttons. In fact my Master made me remove the standard brass tabs on my 501's and replace them with silver tabs from the leather crafter he used. I was never allowed to wear brass as a boy. Silver color was the only acceptable way of leather to him.

- Tee shirts: Black or gray colors for Dominant; white for submissive. Shirts may vary with club insignias. Again true "Old Guard" was always black. Gray was used to accent the black tee shirt for the insignia or wording of an organization to appear on the tee shirt.

- Tank tops and sleeveless shirts are permitted in informal settings. Tank tops known as wife beaters were the typical "Old Guard" style white tank top.

- Harness: Leather and/or chain, ½ harness for Dominant; full harness for boy/boi/submissive/slaves. The difference between the half harness and the full harness being only over the shoulder and across the chest was a half harness. A full harness went all the way down and back up through the crack of your ass attaching to the half harness. A

full harness was generally worn only by boys/bois/submissives/slaves. Again "Old Guard" Masters harnesses were always made of full leather. Chains were acceptable accents for the harnesses for boys if they were mixed with leather. The boy's/boi's/submissive's harnesses were sometimes half leather and half chain but the full harness straps went down the front and up the ass were always made of leather. Only the under the arm or over the shoulder strap would be allowed to be of chain and not both pieces of the harness. All-over chain harnesses would be reserved for slaves only. I hope everyone does know that the harness was not a fashion statement but was a way in which you could grab one another and hold a boy/boi/submissive/slave in place or move him around under your control and with a Master/Sir's harness it was used for the boy/boi/submissive/slave to hold on to if they were put in a precarious position and should only be touched upon doing so. We also would sometimes lock ourselves together using ropes, quick clips etc. attached to the o rings. Later in the 80's designs were introduced to replace the o rings used in a harness. Harnesses are still made of a solid leather material so as to hold the weight and help the straps and chains hold their positions.

- Shirts would not be worn over a harness once you were in a leather environment. It you wore a harness it was never to be covered unless you were ashamed of your body and that was one thing any leatherman would never claim to be regardless of their shape. I believe that is why still today there is leather jock and harness still in most of the competitions to show us what they really look like and to keep their bodies open and available for play yet covered enough not to get arrested. Men in harnesses still are one of the hottest leather attire for a leatherman.

- Leather or jean jacket may be worn over a harness if it was worn correctly. Being worn correctly meant it would be covered completely. If it was so cold that one needed to be covered up and not reveal anything to the public. Once in an enclosed environment, they had to be opened and only used in colder temperatures to keep their bodies warm. If it was warm enough, they needed always to be removed when wearing a harness underneath. "Old Guard" wanted the bodies exposed for viewing pleasure as well open to play.

- Leather jackets would be of the biker type with epaulettes. Well today there are many types but it was always considered to be the real leatherman's jacket when they had the epaulettes and the angled zipper with lots of pockets and belted waist so as not to have the cool air go up the body.

- Head gear was reserved for Masters only.

- Mir caps/Covers (aka motorcycle/Trooper Cap) reserved for Dominants.

- Ball cap (leather or jockey cloth) reserved for Alpha/Senior submissive. Only outside in the cold weather would boy/boi/submissive/slaves be allowed to wear a cap only.

- Gloves were reserved for heavy players, glove fetishist, uniforms or motorcycle riders.

    o Only a Master/Sir was allowed to wear gloves.

    A submissive was not allowed to wear them in public. If they needed them for their motorcycle ride they would be allowed but, they would be left with the motorcycle when they parked their bike unlike that of the Master/Sir who would carry them always.

- Vest: The most important item of a leatherman's life. It usually was the first item purchased or given to or by a leatherman. A bar vest usually comes just to the nipple point of a leatherman for a proper fit. It should come to just above the waist line in the back. There are multiple different styles, however for the best fit, is the 7 panel vest in my opinion. A vest can be used for dress or for a pin vest where event pins are kept. There are some men who have protocols on which side local pins go on and other pins are not commingled with local pins so they are kept on the other side of the front panels of the vest. See the Leatherboys' Handbook by Vincent L. Andrews if you're interested in that protocol. Patches of your club or clubs should be worn on the back of this vest. There is nothing wrong with multiple vests as well for myself I have 5 vests. I have 3 pins vest from my long career, and ILSb vest from the year of sponsorship and a dress vest with just my name badge for higher protocol type events. A vest can be worn without anything underneath it or with a t shirt or even a leather shirt. The vest can also be worn over a harness for a more formalized harness look.

- Play scenes were not to be discussed, verbally or written, with outsiders of the community. This was in "Old Guard" tradition like a sin. Due to the times and circumstances of being very private and in our own world. Things like this were never discussed with anyone not into the scene. It was forbidden. It was considered to be a huge violation of not only the people in the scene but a true disgrace to anyone not understanding the lifestyle. This was actually punishable by the council in the old days. A typical punishment was that of not being able to participate in any functions for three months on the first offense. You were not invited to the next three play parties and basically it was looked upon as almost being banned from your group. It was something men just didn't do. Play scenes were considered private. Much like today, many people do not like to have their sexual activities discussed openly. It was the same then, but it was also done for our protection and survival.

- The playspace and toys were always to be maintained by the boy/boi/submissive/slave. This was done for his own protection. He was to sanitize the entire space, wipe all utensils down, cleaning all furniture and floors so as the space would be clean and as sanitized for the next use. If the Master/Sir wanted to use it after a play session whether it be on his boy or another, the boy was always being played with clean toys and objects. If it wasn't clean, there was no one to blame but the boy/boi/submissive/slave that was used last in the play space.

- Outsiders interested in a play scene would be brought in and facilitated to the scene, but only with sincere interests and great discretion after a period of waiting.

- Full leather, or formal leather also known in "Old Guard" as High Cow, was reserved for after 10:00pm and only with our own kind or at special events.

- Always use someone's entitlement before their name – i.e. Master, Sir, Daddy, boy or slave. If you do not know the person, and/or their title, always address as "Sir". A submissive will quickly inform you if that title has not been earned.

- subs would stand with feet set at shoulder width and hands held behind their back resting on the tailbone, aka **parade rest/point position**, with chest out, head bowed communicating submission and pride.

- Never join in a scene uninvited. This was and still is a major taboo. One would be kicked out of a club or community if this was done on more than one occasion. It was not only considered something not done but wasn't acceptable under any circumstances. This is still true today.

- Never talk to anyone in a scene. This will disrupt the scene and the headspace of all parties doing the scene. Possibly even cause danger. If talking was to be done, it was taken out of the dungeon space or spoken very quietly so as to not interrupt anyone's scene in the dungeon. Under no circumstance would you talk to anyone playing.

- Gauntlets were only reserved for Master/Sir's. They were never worn by anyone with a lesser title and certainly not for any boy/boi/submissive/slaves. boy/boi/submissive/slaves were allowed to wear a small right leather wrist cuff.

- Never interrupt a Master/Sir/Top engaged in a scene or during "aftercare" with his boy/boi/submissive/slave.

- Boy's crotches were to be shaved or tightly clipped to show that they were ready for play without worry of being burned/ or have any issues with pubic hair in any way.

- Wear your keys and hankies appropriately. Only on the left if you were a Master/Sir/Top and on the right for all other stations.

- Masters/Sirs/Daddies, and Tops would never wear a collar. Collars are never to be worn as fashion statements or accompanying an outfit because you think it looks hot. Collars serve a purpose; don't misuse the purpose they were intended to mean.

- Don't wear a collar or chain around your neck as a boy/boi/submissive/slave if you are not collared to a Master/Sir. This was a big taboo in "Old Guard" times as it was seen as a fib or lie. If you were not collared you would not wear a collar. If you had a Daddy, dog tags were acceptable. Therefore, wearing a collar that was not worn for the right reason was looked upon as violating the code. If you were not collared to a Master/Sir you were displaying a falsehood or lying.

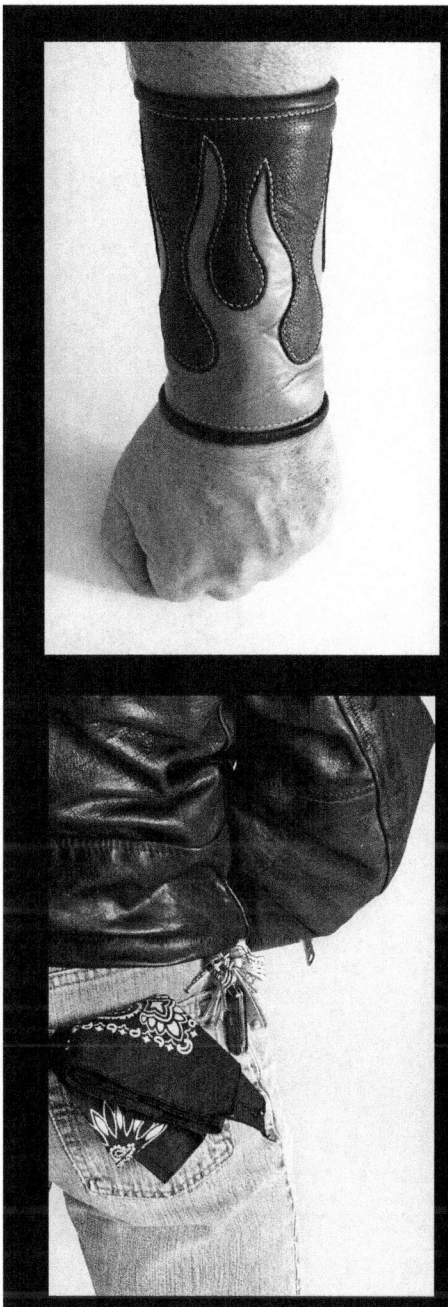

- For boys/bois/submissives/slaves you were to give your life, your body, your heart and your soul in service.

- It was a privilege to serve, honor and obey as a boy/boi/submissive/slave.

- Never interrupt a Master/Sir when he was engaged in conversation. Always say excuse me Master/Sir when interrupting, should it become necessary.

- Men in the scene never discussed or wrote about a scene to outsiders. As many of you know there were lots of pocket novels or fantasy novels but never true accounts of scenes until lately. This was strictly an "Old Guard" taboo.

- "Old Guard" used chain collars for boys/bois/submissives, dog choker collars were used for puppies and leather collars were generally held exclusively for slaves. The heavier the chain usually meant the bigger the commitment. E.g. was in a consideration collar or training collar, or a permanent collar? The permanent collar should be the heaviest of the three collars.

- I don't care how horny you were while watching a scene never grab/fondle/pinch and or touch yours or anyone else's nipples, crotch or ass! This is simply not done! Remember we as "Old Guard" respected one another and wouldn't touch another leatherman unless we were actively participating in a scene or our own boy/boi/submissive/slave.

- If a boy/boi/submissive/slave wants to talk to a Master/Sir and he is a collared boy/boi/submissive/slave, he would ask for permission from his Master/Sir first if he could speak with another Master or Sir. If a boy/boi/submissive/slave wants to speak to someone else's Master/Sir, he would ask that collared boys/boi/submissive/slave prior to speaking to the Master/Sir so that the owned boy/boi/submissive/slave was aware of a discussion going to be had by another boy/boi/submissive/slave with his Master/Sir.

- If a Master/Sir wants to speak to another Master/Sir's collared boy he should ask the Owner of that collared boy permission to speak to him.

- What a Master/Sir puts on his boy/boi/submissive/slave stays on his body until he removes it. Under no circumstances would a boy/boi/submissive/slave remove anything that his Master/Sir put on him. This would include handcuffs and other play toys as well.

- In a bar, a boy was never vocal. He would be like a wall flower. He would stand silently either leaning against a wall enjoying a drink or just standing there in **point position** and await the approach of a Master/Sir/Dominant.

    If he was approached by a Master/Sir, he would then listen and obey, only acknowledging by "yes Sir" and "No Sir". There was not generally a lot of discussion or negotiation until the boy left the bar with the Master/Sir. Boys/bois/submissives/and slaves went into a bar not only for a cocktail but on the hunt for a sexual and possible permanent encounter. Prior to the late sixties, boys knew their position. They would go out looking for sex. There was not near as much promiscuity, as there was in the late sixties and beyond. Gay life was in the closet as was leather life. Relationship and ownership was much more abundant. Even if they were not for a 24/7/365 time period, leather boys sought out to be used by Master/Sirs and Dominants depending on their comfort levels. Remember, during those days, we were fighting for our lives to be kept private and not public. Many of you may not understand all this as you are people from later years when things were and are far more open. We were oppressed in who we were then and our lives were much more private and secluded from the main stream. Even in San Francisco, where gay life was erupting, the leathermen were still very much more closeted.

We were known as freaks and weirdoes and certainly not open to general gay life and society, let alone the general society.

POSITIONS FOR PROTOCOL

- **KNEEL** –there were two types of kneeling plus a **kneel down** position. Then there is the **formal presentation** as well as the **informal presentation**. The difference here is whether the ass is touching the legs or not. In the **formal presentation**, the ass is never resting on the legs. The **Informal presentation** position allows the boy to have a more relaxed kneel by resting on his legs. boy/boi/submissive/slave's back would be straight up in both position, his ass would or would not be resting on one or both knees. In all positions His hands are behind the back with his left hand grasping his right hand at waist height. His head would be bowed and eyes down.

- **Informal Half Present Kneel –** If he wanted the boy/boi/submissive/slave to be on one knee with his ass resting on his legs in a more relaxed environment, he would use the **Informal Half Present Kneel.** The boy would go down on one knee with his ass touching his legs, his back would be vertical with his hands behind his back. His head is bowed and eyes are open to the floor. This can be used in any protocol but was more appropriate in social and low protocols.

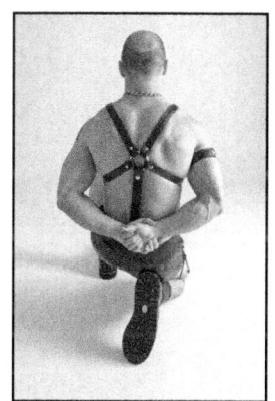

- **A formal half Present position** is where the ass is not touching the legs so the body is straight up from the knees. Here we see the boy is on one knee with his ass **not** resting on his legs his back is vertical with his hands behind his back grasping properly. His head is bowed and eyes are open to the floor. This is a more formal presentation and always used in high protocol.

- **Informal Full Present Kneel –** the boy/boi/submissive/slave would have both knees on the floor placed together. His ass would be resting on both legs. His back is vertical with his hands behind his back grasping properly. His head is bowed and eyes are open to the floor.

- **Formal Full Present Kneel** – the boy/boi/submissive/slave would have both knees on the floor placed together. His ass would not be resting on both legs. His back is vertical with his hands behind his back grasping properly. His head is bowed and eyes are open to the floor.

In both presentations of kneeling, the hands would be behind the boy's back with the left grasping the right hand denoting submission of the right hand. The boy's head would be slightly bowed. The eyes would be open and downward, slightly, not to make full eye contact with the Master/Sir. The main difference in **Half present and Full present** is the location of the knees and a **Formal present and Informal present** is the boy's ass placement, whether or not it he is resting his ass on the legs.

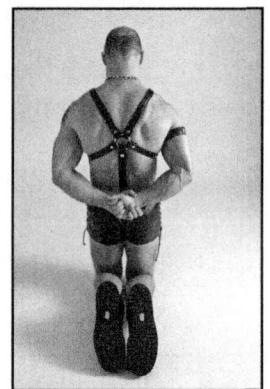

- **KNEEL DOWN** – the boy/slave/submissive kneels facing away from his Master/sir, with knees as far apart as possible, hands flat on the floor in front of him with index finger and thumbs touching to form a triangle, into which he rests his forehead. The chest should be on the floor with the ass high to provide full exposure.

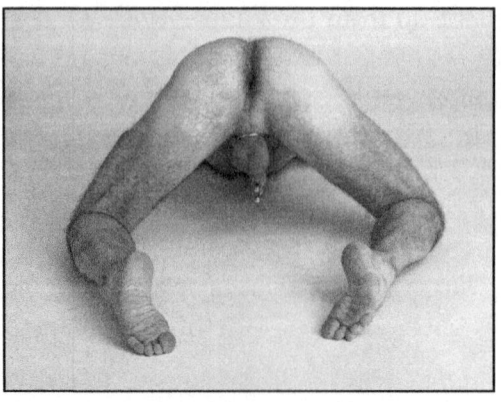

- **PUBLIC PRESENT KNEEL** – if told to kneel in a vanilla public setting, the boy/boi/submissive/slave would do so in such a way as to not draw attention to himself, but as any person might do if no chair were available. Usually this was just both knees on the floor in relaxed position, as a normal person would do if they were going to get down on their knees.

- **STANDING PRESENT** – the boy/boi/submissive/slave would remain standing, not kneeling, with feet together, much like that of an attention in the military, only having his heels touching. Hands are at the side of the boy/boi/submissive/slave, the head bowed slightly with eyes open.

- **PUBLIC PRESENT** position was where the boy/boi/submissive/slave's feet would be spread slightly apart. This is not to be confused with the **Standing Present** where the feet are together. Let me be clear here, **Public Present** was with feet slightly apart **Standing Present** the feet are together. This is the only basic difference between the two. Public present would give the boy/boi/submissive/slave the best possible natural look without being too conspicuous in public. Thus the word Public in Public Present. This position is used a lot in social protocol.

Public present, the boy/boi/submissive slave could stand slightly behind the Master/Sir's right shoulder (if right hand dominant) with his head bowed slightly but with full vision of his Master/Sir while they were in a public environment.

- **ON POINT** position was where the boy/boi/submissive/slave would be at parade rest with feet spread apart. However, here the boy's hands would be behind his back, with the left grasping the right about waist high and head and eyes lowered. Usually this would be done if standing with his Master/Sir. The boy/boi/submissive/slave would stand slightly behind the right shoulder of the Master/Sir he was in service to. If the boy/boi/submissive/slave would just be told to assume the On Point position he would assume this pose wherever told to do so. Whenever a boy/boi/submissive/slave is in doubt on how he should stand, this would be the most acceptable stance for him both publicly and at leather events. This position would show respect, yet allow the boy to be comfortable. In the Military, parade rest or at ease is the term for this position.

- **DEFAULT** position – the boy/boi/submissive/slave would stand slightly behind his Master/Sir shoulder, usually the right side, if the Master/Sir was right hand dominant, and assume one of the above positions. Usually it was the **On Point or Public Present** position, depending what protocol type was being used. Public present would be used for social and low protocols and On Point would be used for High Protocols.

- **REST** – the boy/boi/submissive/slave kneels with both knees on the floor. He rests his ass on his legs. The hands are placed comfortably on the thighs, palms up and the submissive is allowed eye contact. Palms up denotes the boy is available to do whatever he needs to do for his Master/Sir.

Note: if this position becomes too difficult to hold for long periods, the boy/slave/submissive may shift to a Sit Position with his legs spread apart. In High Protocol this position would be used never allowing the Sit Position.

- **SIT Position** – The boy/boi/submissive/slave is permitted to sit comfortably on the floor either at his Master/Sir's feet or within easy reach of his Master/Sir's hands. Eyes are open and at normal position for viewing of his Master/Sir. If hands were open palms up it would be assumed the boy was available to serve at any time. This would only be used in high protocol. In low and social protocol the hands were not important. The boy/boi/submissive/slave could relax his hand gestures appearing to be truly relaxed.

- **SERVE** – food or beverage is served from the left side of the Master/Sir with the right knee down, left leg bent, left elbow on left knee, right elbow in left palm, serving with the right hand. Now this stance has to be understood. Only if the boy is presenting food or beverage. If it has to be served from a bigger plate to the Master's/Sir's plate, the left hand would support the major plate and the right hand would be used for serving to the Master's plate. Head bowed if finished

head semi upward to view the plates and removal of placement of food to the Master/Sirs plate. Serving is always done from the left side. Removal of plates etc. should always be done from the right side of the Master/Sir. This is done for high protocol service.

In low protocol, the boy/boi/submissive/slave would come to the left side and holding the plate or item in the left hand with the right hand under the left supporting the item. If the boy/boi/submissive/slave was to serve he would use the right hand to do it. He is in a **Standing Present** position. Head would be bowed slightly. This would be to serve. The same position to remove plates or items would be done on the right side of the Master/Sir.

When it is time to give the item or plate to the Master/Sir, it would be held away from the boy/boi/submissive/slave's body like giving him the item. Again the item would be in the left hand with the right hand supporting the lift of the item to be served.

The Master/Sir should take the item at that point from the boy/boi/submissive/slave. If it's a plate the boy/boi/submissive/slave should place it in front of the Master/Sir. The boy/boi/submissive/slave would state "Your beer Sir" or "your food Sir" etc. The Master/Sir should respond with at least a "Thank you boy/boi/submissive/slave".

- **BACK PRESENT** – the boy/slave/submissive lies on his back, knees up and spread wide apart. The boys/boi/submissive/slave's hands above his head, fully exposing his genitals and his full body for the Master/Sir to view or use.

- **OTHER PRESENTS** the order "Present" directs a form of kneeling. The order "Present" while pointing to a piece of furniture or equipment directs that the boy/boi/submissive/slave would be bend over it, presenting his ass.

"Back Present" while pointing to a table, couch or bed, directs the boy/boi/submissive/slave to take that position on the table, couch or bed or whatever furniture, using his back as the basis to present. "Present (anything else)" would direct the boy/slave/submissive to make that part of his anatomy exposed and available in the best way he could, understanding and taking the circumstances being in a kneeling present or a back present position.

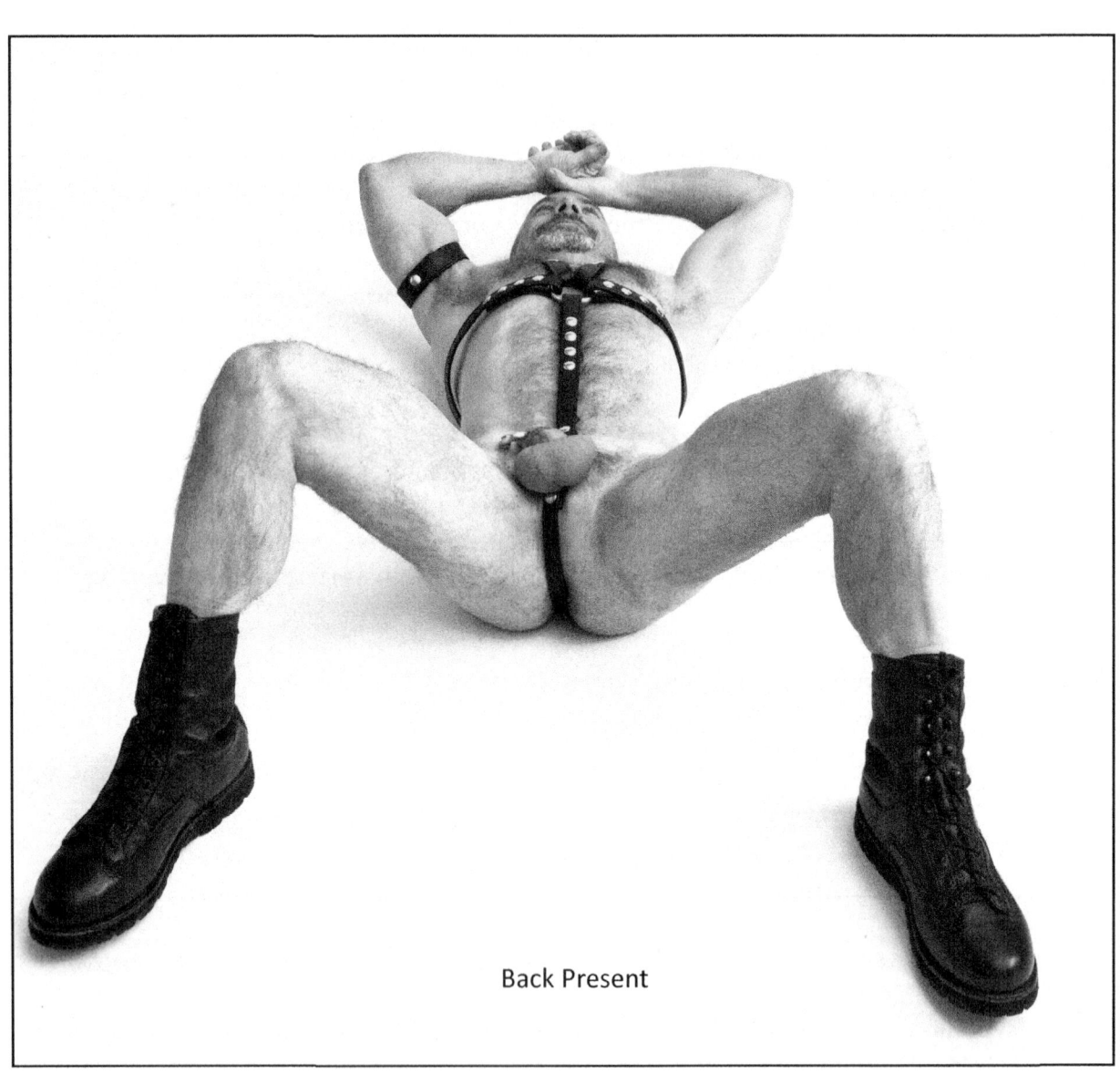

Back Present

- **INSPECTION POSITION (a 3 part presentation)** – the boy/slave/submissive goes to the center of the room and stands facing away from the door, or away from his Master/Sir if he is in the room. The Master/Sir would give him the directive to strip or remain dressed. He would remove all his clothes and fold and set neatly to the right side, if he had been given the directive to strip. If no directive is given, generally it is implied to strip as an inspection position is generally done with no clothes on. Under either circumstance, he would then spread his legs as far apart as possible, while maintaining good balance, placing his hands behind his neck and keep his head straight and eyes forward slightly downward. When given the command "Continue", second part of the inspection, he bends at the waist, putting his hands on the floor or on his knees, if this is not possible. When given the command "Continue" a second time, or the third part of the inspection, he was to assume a kneel-down position. That position is already described above. He would kneel with knees as far apart as possible, hands flat on the floor in front of him with index finger and thumbs touching to form a triangle, into which he rests his forehead. The chest should be on the floor with the ass high to provide full exposure.

HAND AND EYE SIGNALS FOR PROTOCOL

These were used in high protocol if the Master/Sir had previously established them. These signals were vitally important in High protocol as it made the attendance of a boy to his Master/Sir to be that of unspoken words where the boy could be told to do many things. If you were in a leather setting, it was often more pleasing to communicate silently. To avoid confusion, here are a few silent signals I recommend:

- **Stop or silence** – if walking, fold the right arm up to shoulder height, close to the body and display a closed fist. The right hand was used as a signal to the boy/boi/submissive/slave as the right was always the flag side for the boy/boi/submissive/slave. He used the same hand but open fist fingers extended to signal if already stopped and he wished the boy/boi/submissive/ 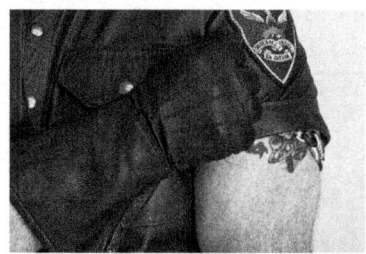 slave to stop speaking or not to start speaking. Nowadays, I have seen similar signals used by regular people, not into leather, as a sign to another person to talk to the hand or stop speaking.

- **Come to me or I want to say something to you** – when entertaining others, or when out in public, the boy/boi/submissive/slave always kept Master/Sir in view. Not only was this critical to maintain hand signals but anytime under any protocol this was always to be observed. A boy in service should never be far from his Master/ Sir. By placing the index and second fingers of  your left hand on your opposite right bicep, the boy/boi/submissive/slave knew to immediately attend you. He would come to the Master/Sir and take an **On Point** position and await his orders.

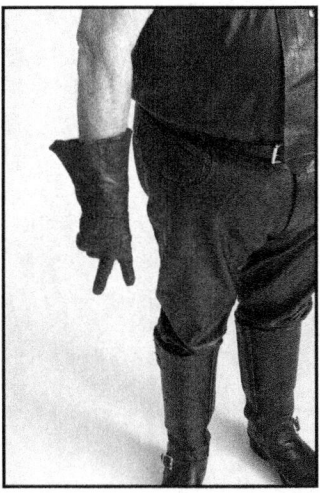

- **Acquire distance** – when in the presence of Leatherman where a conversation was occurring, Master/Sir would motion with two fingers from his right hand below and away from the waist. Again note: the right hand was used, as this was a signal not to be confused with any other hand gesture. The right hand was always the main hand in giving hand signals to a boy/boi/submissive/slave. Now here there seems to be some issues and let me explain. If the boy was close to his Master and in a group sometimes this signal would be a little difficult to see. Therefore, a Master/Sir would always look first to the boy/boi/submissive/slave and once eye contact was made he then would look downward to his right hand as to give the boy an eye contact to observe his right hand and see the signal. Again the boy would have to be in close proximately to observe both the eye and hand signals.

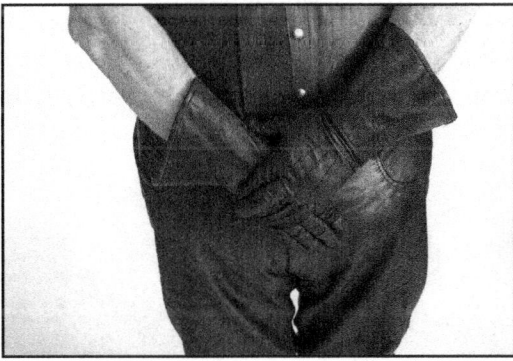

- **Sit** – if Master/Sir desired to have boy/boi/submissive/slave sit, Master/Sir would motion boy/boi/submissive/slave by putting the left index and second finger together crossing over each other and then place the fingers over the top of the right hand.

- **Kneel** – if Master/Sir desired to have boy/boi/submissive/slave kneel, Master/Sir would motion boy/boi/submissive/slave by pointing with the index finger to the floor with the right hand where the boy will kneel on one knee in an upright position. This position was known always to be a **Formal Half Present.** Why **Formal Half Present** instead of **Informal**? Because it was generally used mainly in High Protocol events.

  If he wanted the boy/boi/submissive/slave to be **Formal Full Present** on both knees he would use the index and second finger and point to the floor. Again **Formal** was used due to High Protocol situation.

If an order was given, the boy/boi/submissive/slave would acknowledge it in silence by nodding his head slowly and once only and then leave to execute the order. If no order was given he was to remain there until further ordered in silence or until spoken to. The purpose in presenting oneself was to show respect to the Master/Sir and for the boy to feel his submission, to acknowledge his service, by assuming this humble position.

PROTOCOL FOR NEGOTIATIONS AND WHAT THEY MEAN

When answering any negotiations, the following was what the standard bottom's responses would mean. This became necessary after the computer age as I have said before and in today's world a real necessary thing. Negotiations are meant so each person can agree to honor what has been agreed to take place in the scene. It doesn't mean they have to happen; they are just the parameters to base the play scene on. Once the negotiations are agreed upon prior to the scene beginning, with both parties understanding what will be allowed as well as what won't be allowed. If the scene should go to a "maybe" item, before it starts you must get the bottom's approval. We have to do this now to protect all parties involved. Remember, "Old Guard" didn't do negotiations, we just submitted, admitting to do what we needed to do to please our Master/Sir. It was understood that by their title we could trust and honor that oath they took and knew by their titles what we could possibly expect. Today, we never know what to expect by anyone's title and for that very reason negotiations came into our scenes for all. Here you should understand what the standard negotiations should be. Again, you need to stipulate this prior to the negotiations so everyone understands what they are agreeing to and what it means not to agree to do.

Yes – Interested and willing to do it. This means the bottom or top has agreed to allow this type of play, not that it has to happen but it is ok to do this type of play.

Maybe – A Possible, with negotiation, or with time and increased trust levels which needs to be established. If a Master/Sir should decide to choose to do a maybe in the negotiations, he must secure the approval prior to moving forward in this type of play. This must be done as it may not be a comfort level or something that the boy/boi/bottom feels safe doing with that Master/Sir. Again, they may feel the Master/Sir is good at it and yet they haven't built the trust to allow this play, so still the answer then might be "no, not at this time". Maybe is always something we have to be careful about in these days when people can be held liable for their actions in BDSM. If it's not done with consent, you then have an issue to overcome and be legally liable. One of the major ones I can think of is barebacking or fluid bonding. It may come in time due to the parties involved but right away it may be something the boy/boi/bottom isn't willing to do the first time they submit. They need to get to know the Master/Sir and feel comfortable and fully understand the repercussions when they are not involved or horny in a scene, as this can sometimes determine someone's response and later they are sorry for giving the ok. The Master/Sir should also understand this when they are asking for this type of play. What they are asking could be misconstrued under sexual excitement and not be a correct answer. I can't state this strongly enough today as infections are occurring due to the heat of the moment but afterward they realize what they have done and then feel they have been abused or misused, which can open up liability to the Master/Sir.

No – No interest at all, not for anyone at any time. This response has to be respected and if it should be done against the boy/boi/submissive's consent, you could be held liable in a court of law.

Unfortunately today, we have come to being held liable for these actions and possible abuse repercussions in our play. This just makes it more important that you find a good person to play with that understands all of this and you need to understand that when the negotiations are done, you are responsible for your actions; each party has the responsibility then to uphold their end.

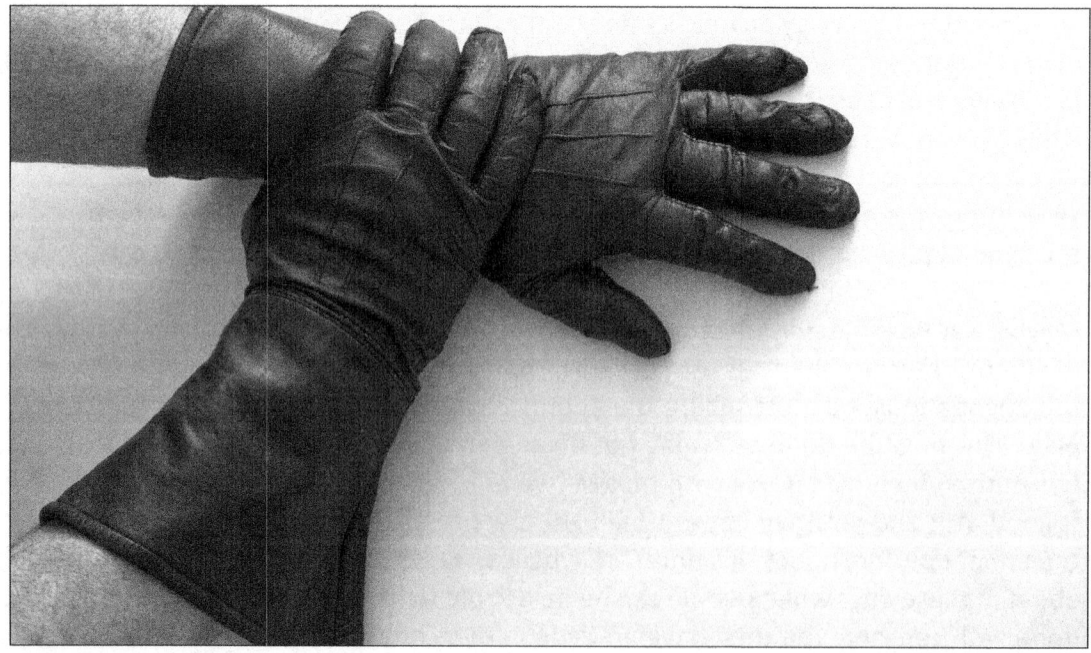

DUNGEON PROTOCOLS

Dungeon rules at this point are something that everyone should know backward and forward and would be the next thing everyone should put to memory. What I have included here are basics and there may be many additional ones which the individual dungeon may request of their participants. This can be either regionally or for some special reason ie; pansexual verses all gay. Dungeon rules are needed again for the newbie as well as the old person as to make sure strict and steadfast rules apply to all. This promotes a good and equitable dungeon for all to play in promoting a safe, sane and consensual arena for people to have fun in.

1. Always bring everything you need for your scene with you. Should you forget something, ask the Dungeon Monitor for any item you have forgotten and they will try to aid in securing that item. There is no guarantee though they will be able to help.

2. If you are unsure of anything, ask the Dungeon Monitor (DM) quietly, if play is in progress in the Dungeon.

3. Do not interfere with anyone's scene. You could watch but stand far enough away and do not talk or discuss anything regarding that scene as when a sub is blindfolded or bound, their senses are more aware of things going on around them. If you are invited into the scene you may join in the scene but do so as quietly as possible and only if you're invited!

4. DO NOT touch or talk to a sub during or after a scene, unless asked to do so. Touching or talking to a sub on the edge of sub space, even with the best of intentions, can ruin their whole night as well as the scene. This applies to the Master/Sir as well.

5. DO NOT talk to, or distract, a Master/Sir during a scene. Their job is to concentrate on their sub and what they are doing! Likewise, do not stand near to scene and

chatter, which can be distracting for both Dom and sub! There will be chill out areas where you can chat away without disturbing anyone. (In the separate space not the Dungeon.)

6. DO, however, feel free to talk to people who are not involved in a scene out of the Dungeon area. This is a great way to meet new people; learn new techniques; check out new equipment; ask for help etc. The vast majority of people are happy to help and advise when asked at the appropriate time. Do allow people time to relax and 'come down' after they have been playing however. It is called aftercare.

7. DO NOT walk between a Master/Sir and a boy/boi/submissive/slave while corporal punishment is taking place. Whips, floggers and canes etc. are designed to hurt; you will not be where they are meant to land and you could end up being seriously hurt! Likewise be very careful if you need to walk behind a Master/Sir as he was swinging back. If you are hit accidentally, you have ONLY yourself to blame. Do remember that a 6 foot whip is still 6 foot long on the backswing plus the Master/Sir's arm throwing it.!

8. NO alcoholic drinks and cigarettes etc were allowed in the dungeon scene. Cigar play if available will usually be outside in a private space. Leather outfits worn were and are very expensive and/or specially made, their owners REALLY do not want holes burned in them or drinks spilt over them!

9. If fire play was allowed in the dungeon, be sure the DM knows you're going to do it so he can have the fire extinguisher and special equipment available if you are not prepared.

10. If Wax play was also allowed in the dungeon, ask the DM if they have tarps for you to drop should you wish to play with wax and didn't bring your own. Do not do wax play if you don't have a tarp to protect the equipment and floor.

11. DO check with the Dungeon Master FIRST if you feel concern about how someone else playing. What is too much for you, may be just a warm up for them!

12. DO NOT touch other people's equipment, clothes, toys, etc. If you want to look at or borrow something, always ASK first after the scene was over or prior to, but be sure the sanitation wasn't voided. And make sure you return it promptly afterwards!

13. DO remember that being submissive, whether alone or not, doesn't mean being available for anyone who describes themselves as Master/Sir. If you wanted to play with someone, ask them politely and accept whatever their answer is BEFORE you touch etc. If a submissive is with someone, you should politely approach whoever they are with, first. If either says no, that does NOT mean you should keep trying! Remember to negotiate your scenes in public spaces. If someone won't stop bothering you, report it to the Dungeon Monitor and allow him or her to deal with it.

14. DO NOT lounge around and sit on the bondage benches and dungeon furniture. If you were sitting on the equipment, you were preventing someone else from using it for its intended purpose!

15. DO feel free to watch a scene in public dungeons. The people involved were aware that they were in a public dungeon and didn't mind you watching. It was a very good way to learn new techniques and get some ideas of how the various implements were used. However, just watch, don't join in unless invited.

16. DO play at your own level. There was no prize for whoever plays hardest! There are very good reasons, & absolutely no shame, in playing lightly if that was what you want to do.

17. DO have a drink ready for your sub to drink during and after the scene was over. Many subs find playing very dehydrating, having the drink ready means you did attend to their thirst as part of the scene's aftercare. It also means you could send your sub to the bar to fetch the drinks!!!

18. If you MUST Play with or touch yourself while watching a scene, and you are going to cum, cum in your pants – not on the players or spectators. Keep your privates to yourself.

19. NO drugs were or are permitted as it changes the body makeup for play.

20. Poppers were approved if consent was given by the participating parties.

21. If blood sports were being practiced, be sure to dispose of all instruments in proper containers. Be sure the space is sanitized before someone else uses the same space.

22. Remember, that when a scene ends there is aftercare for both parties. Be sure you do so and make sure your sub was not forgotten about. Give them the time and space to care for one another. Be sure they are able to function properly

before leaving them alone. Do not interrupt aftercare as it is as important as the actual scene.

23. Safe sex was recommended and endorsed. This is a decision to be made by the people involved.

24. DM'S RULE THE DUNGEON OBEY THE DM (Dungeon Monitor)! No matter whom you may be or think you were or are, the DM overrules everyone.

25. IF someone who is deaf is in play, the dungeon area where this play was to be performed must be lighted enough for visual sight for communication, as the deaf party could not hear anything in the play scene. Both parties must have a way of communicating either with sign language or some other type of communication.

26. Never leave your submissive alone. If you had to leave for some reason, bring in someone you trust to oversee your submissive until you return.

27. Always clean up after you have finished your scene. Be sure to leave all equipment sanitized as well as cleaned as to not promote spread of disease.

28. Do not monopolize a play area or equipment. Allow yourself a time limit so others could enjoy the same equipment.

I,_____ - understand Dungeon Protocol and agree to follow the dungeon rules while at the party.

_____ Please check here if you do not want to be in any photographs. I understand that I must wear this badge to identify myself as someone who didn't want to have my picture taken and be identified as such in silence.

This final statement should be followed by any public dungeon and badges should show the proper notations. Be respectful of those notations. Be sure anyone taking pictures is aware of the notations and what they mean.

BOY'S BILL OF RIGHTS

These rights are for boys, not for slaves, as all this should be covered in the slave's contract prior to his signing. However gross misuse of any of these can be considered abuse and can if pushed be punishable by law.

1. Every boy has the right to have his body, intellect, and emotions protected by his Dom.

2. Every boy has the right to choose the man whom he serves and to discontinue that service and take his leave without being subjected to physical, mental, or emotional abuse.

3. Every boy has the right to be cared for, disciplined appropriately, and allowed to feel pride in his submission.

4. Every boy has the right to protected sex if he so wishes. This is a choice be sure you know what you want before your questioned.

5. Every boy has the right to privacy if he so wishes. No boy can be blackmailed, publicly humiliated, or physically coerced into service without his expressed desire to be so.

6. Every boy has the right to defend himself from physical, sexual, and emotional abuse.

7. Every boy has the right to consent or not to consent to sexual activities. This needs to be done in the negotiations to avoid complications.

8. Every boy has the right to seek refuge, counsel, and advice from other subs and Doms without the expectation of sex, money, or any other service in return.

9. Every boy has the right to a physically and emotionally available circle of friends.

10. Every boy has the right to protect his own possessions and finances against intercession, theft, and non-consensual acquisition. Key words here are non-consensual.

LEATHERMAN'S CODES AND CREEDS

This leatherman's code was used as a basis for many "Old Guard" leathermen. Many clubs used it as the oath or the code to join their club. This code became well known in the early 60's until the late 80's. Now this code has almost disappeared!

HONOR: I will form a bond with other Leathermen. In my associations, I will not lie, cheat or steal. Nor shall I malign my brothers in leather. I will pay due respect to all and shall, at all times, settle any and all disputes with discretion. I shall always respect their privacy and property!

INTEGRITY: I will engage only in activities that are personally known and experienced by me. I will personally test and experience any unknown activities prior to engaging in any play with others.

TRUST: I will not misrepresent my abilities to others. I will establish and abide by set rules of conduct and will always act in the best interests of all parties in any and all situations. I will not abuse the trust earned and placed in me by my brothers in leather.

TEMPERANCE: I will recognize the endurance and limits of others. I will not use or apply any instrument of pain and/or discomfort to others, in any manner that may exceed reasonable or agreed upon limits. Nor shall I use any instrument that shall cause deliberate or unnecessary damage to the mind or body, nor any that shall be a danger to others.

When the Safe, Sane and Consensual leathermen's creed came into existence this code had some changes. This leathermen's creed along with R.A.C.K., Risk Aware Consensual Kink, creed grew greatly. This happened especially after the computer age when we had to realize the experience levels of Masters/Sirs were not where they use to be prior to this age. We also could not trust in the titles of a person to uphold that amount of knowledge. Some clubs abandoned it and took the new Leatherman's creeds as their new oath for members. The old leathermans' code has almost disappeared for these reasons!

THE "OLD GUARD" HIERACHY

COUNCIL

The council, which was a group of Elders of the community, really governed the local leather community. They were a board of directors, so to speak, for the community. The Council pretty much set the regulations and such in which the clubs/organizations would function within the community and with each of the other clubs. The Council was made up of senior members from each of the local clubs each having equal representation on the Council.

The council group established all the rules, what clubs were governed by the council, and defined the punishment when someone made a violation. It was with their approval that everything would happen within our club and probably most of our dwellings, dungeons, and lives. In "Old Guard" days we had our council which for us had members from several groups to govern the San Francisco Bay area. They met monthly as I remember for about 2 hours just to let each group know what was going on with the other and to cross communicate and populate the clubs. It was at this meeting of the council, that the information of other clubs would be filtered down to the clubs and then to the members. All coverings for Masters had to be approved by this council so the clubs around recognized the Masters. All other ceremonies would be club controlled and that information would then be passed around at the council meetings giving the council knowledge of who had been received what titles within the said community. It really brought the 3 "S" together to give us the strictness, structure and stability that was so prevalent in our organizations. In today's world this probably would be the clubs and organizations out there. Unfortunately the clubs and organizations out there generally don't meet together anymore to keep each club in the general area informed. This is where the breakdown of the council has appeared. I believe if we could revive this, it would cut down on so much of the bickering and feuds amongst communities and clubs. The council would act as the mediator for grievances to be handled amongst the clubs and or its members.

ELDER

Who and what was an elder? Well the elders were usually one of the 7-9 members of the community who were the longest living members and only upon death or moving from the community would their seat on the council become available. To gain access to the council, you had to be within the community many years and really it was done on a pecking order not a voting order by age and seniority as well as a member of good standing within the local community/group. I remember being brought in front of the council by my Master who was an Elder of our community and a council member.

As a member of the council, when I was brought forth, he had no say in my acceptance. I had to prove myself to the council and within the community for a period of one year prior to being accepted into the community. After the one year period of dedication to my club all the other members of the club voted to grant me the right to use the patch of my community; this vote had to be approved by the council. My Master had no say so in that vote nor could he do anything with me at any of the social or play parties for my pledge period unless I didn't have to serve the Council or the Elders. I served Him daily but when it came to a social or play party, I was given the privilege of serving the council and or elders other than Master and to be guided by them through the parties and such to gain their approval. When the event was over, I was returned to my Master for his guidance and daily use.

It was considered a privilege to be a part of this elite group and being able to serve the Council or an Elder was the only way you became a member of good standing to the community. This was strictly a service position. It was through that service the community grew and prospered. There was never any question to a Council or Elder's order. It was just expected to be carried out to the best of your ability and would be supervised by that Elder or Council. If you made a mistake you were corrected in front of the council members and you would go on to learn what it was you had to achieve. If you didn't achieve all the orders set forth in that year you were not accepted into the group or given an extended period of privileged service to gain favor. If you still didn't get accepted you were banned from the socials parties and events.

GRAND MASTER

A Grand Master is someone who has attained the true title of Master and has been around in the community holding the title of Master for about 20 years plus, give or take depending on the local leather community. The community wishes to recognize this person as being a long time member of the community and their dedication to the lifestyle through events, education and mentoring. This title is the second highest in the community only one higher is the elder. Again, due to the limited elders in a community, it does vary by the community. The Grand Master is like a Master in waiting to be an Elder. It is from this group that the next in line comes to replace the death or relocation of an Elder from their Community. In some smaller communities this title is never awarded because the community is so small that the community can't offer this due to the sheer numbers of community members. Remember, these are members of the leather community who are totally out in every way demonstrating their Master skills in education, mentoring and community service.

MASTER

To gain the title of **Master**, you had to be within the leather community for over 10 years and have achieved at least 15 levels of play proficiently. These ten years can consist of any title here listed as well. So for example you may be a submissive/slave/ or boy for 5 years a Sir for 5 years achieving your ten years of community service. This was rarely done as this would be classified today as a fast track type of person. In Old Guard Days, no one ever really fast tract anywhere. I for example served my Master for 7 years as a boy, was a Sir for 11 years, and then was awarded my Master's cover. We were all to satisfy our various positions slowly graduating up to the next title. A superior level of dominant play or type of play would be classified as a good and safe player. You needed to be effective in performing various types of play with the understanding what it does to your submissive/bottom. You also needed to show you knew all the first aid of that type of play, i.e. in blood sport play how do you stop a cut from bleeding after normal clotting time. One also had to have achieved the title of Sir first by the community prior to being so considered and titled as a Master. You were expected to understand all the issues and errors that can be made which can cause a bad scene. You had to demonstrate great control. Last but not least be visible in the community and participate in fundraisers.

A level of play would be classified as a flogging, whipping, bondage, wax play, fire play, etc. A Master would have had to perform these levels of play publicly at events held by a group which in the end was supervised by the elders of the community. Upon achieving a level of play, it would be noted by the council. Then you were given a new type of play by a council member for you to achieve and become proficient in. This process would go on until you had achieved 15 types of play noted by the council.

Once you thought you were proficient in that type of play, you were then asked to publicly present that type of play to achieve council approval. Another level of play would be given to you by a council member that night if you had achieved their approval and you could have your next type of play ready at the earliest at the next run, event or party that was supervised. However, rarely would you be ready to present that new type at the next run, event, or party. You had whatever time you needed to accomplish and perfect each type of play. It didn't have to be performed at the very next play party. In fact, the council didn't want you to do that as it was thought you were trying to achieve greatness quickly. They didn't like men who tried to do that. They would generally shoot you down if they saw you were trying to fast track you way to a Master's title. Most of the council members felt only with time were you worthy of such a title. When you were ready to present, you would notify the council and someone from the council would supervise that evening and would watch your scene. There was no given time limit to achieve any type of play given.

There were generally 12 events/parties a year and the # 15 was never achieved in one year. It may take years to achieve 15 levels of play effectively for the council approval. Being that this was the highest title, you had to be far more effective and proficient than when the council gave you your Sir title. During your Sir title years, you would have had to be very visible in the community at leather events donating time and treasure for the community to grow. You had to show a continuation of growth and in control over this time and truly become a pillar on which the community could draw upon.

Once all this was achieved however, the council would hold a meeting and bring you forth amongst all the members and award the title of Master to you through a cover ceremony. It was at this point you would surrender your title of Sir and be known as Master. In "Old Guard" tradition only Masters were allowed to wear covers in public. It was not about the look it was about your accomplishments that you were able to show who and what you knew by this cover. It was also assumed by the council that you would begin teaching or mentoring other Sir's so they could achieve the level of Master within the community. Remember, it is not only about play, but also about control, and performance in community service and many other things that would entitle you to this level of greatness and Title.

This was not an easy title to achieve, as they were very careful about awarding this title just to anyone. It had to be a member of good standing in the community, having done all the community service and attending almost all the meetings and play parties participating in everything they did as well. It was much easier to be awarded the Title of Sir than to be awarded the Title of Master and for that reason a Master was always looked up to as one of the highest members of the community locally and once awarded that title locally you would be viewed nationally at events and play parties with that respect. If you violated that respect, generally word was sent back to your local counsel and the elders would meet and see if any reprimand or removal of title was necessary. It was much stricter then than it is now for most of this has sort of gone to the wayside. Many communities still function with a small hierarchy but they don't really have the power that was around in the "Old Guard" days. We have lost this structure which was so critical to our lives and the rank of our communities that the men of the war were so use to dealing with. The Military took their ranks and titles seriously and so did the "Old Guard" leathermen.

During the cover ceremony a Sir would be given his Cover (a traditional motorcycle cap) by a council member. It is also here where the person receiving the cover understands that he must be governed by those responsibilities of the Master title. He also must understand by taking this cover, the responsibility of a Master is passed. This is a serious responsibility and one has to understand it all before he accepts this cover. It is here when the council felt you were ready to receive it would the cover be given and not before in "Old Guard" tradition.

Remember also in "Old Guard" traditions, we had to gain our Sir title by first being a boy in service to a Master/Sir. This helped us to understand that role, understand what privileges' it granted, and how to properly treat a boy who was in service to you. Having done that, we were expected to have built those foundations for each title from a boy all the way up to a Master. This was generally a basic requirement in order to gain the true title of Master amongst the council. The council and local community were able to witness a major part of your growth as a person and within the leather community and see how you were trained before anything would have been done to award the title of a Master, or any title to you. Now you can see why Masters hold the highest regard within the community amongst all "Old Guard" Leathermen. It was truly a great accomplishment with lots of respect from boys all the way up to the Sir's who help make you the man you now were. Each of us who gained that title all had a special camaraderie as well with the other Masters. Like a select club amongst the elite in leather clubs across the United States.

It has been a long emotional journey for me having to overcome the death of Master as a boy then going on to gain the respect of a community, be covered by that community. Once achieved the Master title, leave that community moving to another before I settled into the Fort Lauderdale. There having been given the title and cover by a different community, I had to show that I was entitled to this title to my new community. I did that by owning a leather store, writing a newsletter monthly for the community, doing demo's publicly, doing educational classes, participating in clubs, fund raisers, and events and allowing many to play and be mentored under my cover. This helped me gain the recognition, that I now have, and I am proud and honored to have. Since I have retired, I am doing some travel back to towns from my journey as well as other places where I have really seen what respect and honor means amongst many leatherfolk. Now, for that reason and for all of those people who gave me that respect, I am proud to be able to write this book sharing my information with all of you as Master John.

SIR

The **Sir** title was given upon achieving the mentorship of first being a daddy, learning all the things about the community at hand. At this time usually you would have mentored a boy or two as their daddy to begin their leather journey. You would have achieved at least three levels of play and performed them publicly, and in front of the council to their liking. You would also now be a dominant and a top at this point. You would have served a period of time as a boy in service to a Master or a Sir. Being a boy was part of the training to help you understand what a boy would go through as well as what the different types of play felt like.

It was stated that a Sir needed to know exactly how it felt to be in service but also to understand what the types of play were and how they were administered. It was considered to be the stepping stone to becoming a good Sir. It help you understand how hard to hit or not to hit, understand all the types of play that were out there and what would turn you on. It also taught you how to be cared for after play. You learned about endorphins and what these rushes were and how it felt to be in that state of mind. It taught you about being dominated and what it meant for that to happen to you and from you. It was a time of great learning. The council believed that to learn how to serve was needed at all the other levels of your journey. Even great Elders served their community and should receive some feelings of commitment and service to his community. Some boys never moved up the ranks as they loved being in service to a man. They would receive great pleasure out of serving both sexually and emotionally. This was also good for not every man needs to be a top nor a Sir or even a Master. "Old Guard" Leathermen felt this was the only way that a Master/ Sir would rise and understand all that their future boy was going through. It was also at this time when one would consider their life, the rewards it has being in service, along with the commitment to leather life and to everything else that once has to commit to when moving up the ranks. As in the military, not everyone becomes a five star general. We still needed the privates and corporals, etc. It takes all great men to do their jobs to make a great army and the council looked at this much the same. It took all levels of titles in leather to make for a great leather community. Once you accomplished all this, and you decided you wanted to go up the ranks of leather, your leather family would give you a gauntlet ceremony to start your Sir journey. You would usually discuss this prior to making the commitment to move up in ranks with your leather family and friends as well as doing a soul searching for what you wanted to give and get from the leather community. This was usually asked by the council at some point in this journey prior to your acquiring your Sir title. So you see it was a major decision. Not everyone wants nor accepts these levels of commitments. Some people just want sex and that is ok, but a great leather community even today has great commitments by all leather people in that community at all titles.

A gauntlet ceremony was a grand celebration whose details will be discussed a little further into this book under the ceremony section. It was at this ceremony, where a gauntlet was given to the new Sir as a symbol of the family's support and love and of his achievements as a dominant top surviving his mentorship as a boy. This was a recognized council title and one which leathermen took very seriously as it truly was a level of distinction to be called a Sir! Many men would choose never to go beyond being a Sir again depending on their commitments to the community and their lives and loved ones. It was during this time served as a Sir that the council would look for the great members of the community to seek out the ones to train to become in training to go for the next title of Master. It took lots of mentoring as a Sir before making that commitment to move up the ranks. You also had to display greatness, control and power within yourself and around yourself. You had to show the community not only were you worthy of being a Sir, but if deciding to move up the ranks to become a Master. So you see this was a time of self development and growth. A time of introspection. A time of searching through your soul for what you felt you wanted. Also a time of commitment to the community and what it did for you and what you did for it.

As you can begin to see here, both the cover and gauntlets were coveted by each individual who wore these articles of attire. The gauntlet, worn on the left arm only, represented the love of his leather family and the cover represented the status of his Title of Master in the community. Both were achievements and accomplishments as well as the acceptance of the responsibilities of the title. They were worn proudly by each member who was awarded his gauntlet and cover respectively. However, over time, the gauntlet and its ceremony have lost its significance and nowadays both Sirs and Masters tend to receive covers. I have even seen submissive with them as they think it is part of the leather uniform. This was never the case in "Old Guard" days, as the cover right off that submissive/boy upon entering any establishment.

Many people today wear these items as a fashion statement. Unfortunately this takes away so much of the symbolism of achievement and accomplishment of what the "Old Guard" symbols meant. They are readily available in retail leather stores and in many colors and designs etc. which have taken on all new meanings in my eyes. People who buy their own gauntlets and covers usually don't have knowledge of all of the traditions and ceremonies. They usually are self-made titleholders and I'm not talking about contest winners. Those titles didn't come around until the late 70's. However, to us "Old Guard" men, Master and Sir still represent these meanings. When you meet an "Old Guard" leatherman who is wearing his gauntlet and cover, he has earned the right to wear them, and a whole new level of respect should be given to him. An Old Guard Acronym for Sir = SERVICE, INTELLIGENCE and RESPECT.

DADDY

Daddy is a title that is also earned and recognized by the council. Most people however think just because someone is older, they are a Daddy. This is a fallacy. Daddies are not always a fuck top role either. Daddies are usually older than their counterpart. Someone who is 30 could be a daddy to a 20 yr old and so on. Yes they are older and should be more worldly, but isn't a 30 year old more worldly than a 20 year old? Generally, yes, they are. Daddies are more mentors on life and situations of life and would be more like a father. Daddies don't always have to be sexual; they can be strictly a mentor/educator. Daddies are usually responsible for the welfare of a boy or group of boys. In leather, they are usually the ones who start the bottom's journey, giving to the boys the basic education on respect, etiquette and protocol training that is required to enter into the title of boy. Prior to being recognized by the council boys were just known as a bottom. Daddy's generally are never lost from a boy's life even after a boy is taken by his Master or Sir.

Daddy's generally don't collar the boys, as this is a privilege reserved for ownership. I have however known some Daddy's who have collared the boys in my life during their training period. A Daddy collaring would not be recognized by "Old Guard" Standards however. In "Old Guard" ways it was customary for the Daddy to give their boys their Dog Tags as a symbol of their family. The dog tags was the symbol to any Master/Sir that this boy was not collared but had been somewhat trained by a Daddy. Much like in the military you got your dog tags when you were starting in the service as a private. The Master/Sir would be able to see that the boy had dog tags. From the dog tags the Master/Sir, when cruising the boy, would know they had some training and were not novices in Leather. The Master/Sir would then know that he could expect some protocol and training and not just be some guy looking to get fucked. They also would expect a little higher play from them, which would make them more desirable to take the boy/boi/submissive/slave home for service and use not just a fuck or a bottom.

This was really the role of the Daddy to prepare the boys for their journey in leather life. Help them grow and deal with issues that they didn't understand either in regular life or in leather life. You also have to remember back in the "Old Guard" day's many of us would lose our families when we came out of the closet as a gay man. Daddies sort of filled that father figure we would miss when we lost our real fathers. The helped mentor us to become men in many ways as you now hopefully understand. This still happens today and when you meet a real Daddy, hopefully you will now know what purpose they serve in that boy's life or boys' lives. They are truly needed and part of our leather culture and life.

DOM'S

Senior Dominants'

Senior Doms as they were called were people who were dominant/aggressive men. These men were usually proficient in some type of play but were always a fuck top. They would not be a switch. They just had some training in play but would always play the power side of the power-submissive role therefore being the Dominant. This is a confusing title but truly is something that once you understand that dominance is about power and not sex it really helps define these groups of men. I'm not saying they are not sexual, I'm just stating for them it was more about the power than the position in sex. Being a Senior Dom meant that you had more training than your counterpart of Junior Dom which is also a title referring to the power exchange to that of a submissive.

Junior Dominants'

Junior Doms were the true beginning of the power exchange roles. Unlike that of tops and we will discuss that next, Junior Dominants were people who understood the Dominant submissive roles and what that does in the overall picture and growth to become a Master/Sir. You could be a Junior Dominant and tell someone in a power exchange that you wanted their cock in your ass and the power and control of the scene as far as the power exchange of the scene was present by having the submissive insert his cock into your ass. The dominance wasn't so much about the sexual position but the power of controlling the submissive's position. Top and bottom were only the position and the two terms used in regular gay life defining which position we enjoyed in sex.

In the day where we were all at different levels of play and there were differences between a leather wearing man and a BDSM play scene man, titles helped define who we were and where we were in our journey as leathermen and as gay men.

I know by now you must really begin to understand that there were many titles in those early days but they were truly used to define who and where you were in the journey. It helped one understand that there is a difference between a top, dominant, daddy, Sir and Master. It clarified who you were to a submissive/boy/slave/bottom, which names define the other side to each of the other roles. But in the world of BDSM and in "Old Guard", your title truly defined who you were and what you were looking for.

TOP

The title of top is usually just that. He is a man who is the aggressive fucker top type of person. Yes in leather, they usually are more dominant than the counter bottom however, they do not posses any real training other than they like to be on top during sex or be the aggressor in sex. The word top was also in regular vanilla gay life and looked at as the same a fucker not a fuckee. There are two types of tops back in the "Old Guard" days and they were known as a Junior Top and a Senior Top. The difference here is the Senior Top just had more knowledge of the leather community than the Junior Top.

A Junior Top was someone who simply enjoyed being the fucker who may switch from time to time but preferred to be on the top. A senior top was one who was strictly a top aggressive fucker and maybe naturally dominant in his overall attitude in life and in sex but had not acquired any skills in leather. The council never recognized these titles. They were just used by people who showed interest in leather as well as vanilla or regular gay life and knew they had to have a title to announce their preference in sex to be welcomed into the leather community. These titles didn't necessarily mean they wanted to be in the leather community. It was like a starter position for them in the gay leather community. And if they were not into leather it just defined them as to what they wanted in sex. It kind of still holds true today, I hear are you a top or a bottom and in some of the websites they ask that question just that way.

To their amazement however, to join the leather community they would have to bottom as a boy before becoming a Sir, which sometimes stopped them from progressing in the leather community as some men felt they were only going to be a top and nothing was going in the out hole. A top is only called by his name with no Sir or Master in front of it.

Now here is an interesting fact: today in pansexual leather folk play, Top and bottom refer only to play positions in scenes. It is a generic term of the two ends of the spectrum in play. If I was a pansexual top I would want to be the one administering the play and the bottom is someone who would receive the play with no power exchange, sex or service. It is strictly a play position. I believe this is one of the reasons why gay leathermen are uncomfortable in a pansexual dungeon. Gay leathermen tend to combine sex with play, which is usually not allowed in pansexual dungeons.

Boy/boi

This title was one that was recognized by the council. From this point forward I will just refer to a boy/boi as "boy". However, boy is the true male boy where boi refers to the female submissive. The term boi also was used instead of boy for the boi who is castrated which again represents a more feminine male or boy not able to have his body make testosterone. Also this term is used for the transgender boi. It can also be use for the one choosing to be the other sex either through just mindset or through physical alteration of their body parts.

This title was awarded to a person wanting to become part of the leather community. First the boy/boi/submissive/slave might get a collar of consideration, then a training collar and after months or even years might earn his permanent collar. In my day, everyone started a true leather life as a boy or a slave. We had to work our way through this time understanding the headspace, terminology, protocol and techniques and learn all that we had to do in our leather life ahead. It was critical for each person at that time to go through this time so one would understand the words "in service". Here we learned our bootblacking, leather care, and were either chosen by a Master or Sir or given to a daddy to train us and make us ready for a Master or Sir.

In my case my Master had chosen me to start this journey with him specifically. When I met him, I was not aware of all that I had to do so this became a critical step for me on my journey. I firmly believe this is where the foundation was built for who I am today and for what I stand for. I really still believe anyone who wants a true leather journey life should spend some time in service to a Master or Sir to fully understand what it means to be a boy. Also what does a boy go through on a daily basis, some of the frustrations, disappointments, excitement, and honor to be in that position. For me a boy is someone who is cherished, loved and nurtured. A great boy is a gift from God.

Many "Old Guard" Masters say the word love should never be spoken in a Master/Sir/boy/boi/submissive/slave type of relationship. I do not subscribe to this theory, as I was indeed loved. For me it was because of that love I surrendered to his whips and needs becoming all the boy I could be. Yes, it was an honor to serve My Master and I felt privileged to have that honor and still consider it an honor to have served him. I did it, though, because I so loved him. Without that love, I would have never taken the first steps to do this journey. I now look back and thank God that this happened to me. Now, I am able to share this information with you. I believe had I not loved him I would not have cherished this journey as I have and become what I have because of his love returned. I understand that the word love in leather changes things. I have also seen how a boy can take advantage of the word love. So one has to be very careful when using that word in a leather relationship as it tends to let a boy forget his duties or he thinks he can get away with something because you love him. So should this happen to you be careful. If you should love him make sure you maintain all the other steps or protocol and training so he will understand that you love him because he does what he is suppose to do in service.

The rights of a boy were as follows; the boy had to do as his Master/Sir demanded/ordered. These orders were usually verbal or written and given to the boy on a daily basis. The boy had to stand at the dominant side of his Master/Sir either equal or one step behind the Master/Sir. This was usually determined during the protocol introduction of the particular Master/Sir.

Being a boy also had some rights which do not apply to a slave. The boys rights are listed later on in this book. The boy may express his feelings or needs to his Master/Sir however, the Master/Sir does have the right to override the boy's feelings or comments and go with whatever the Master/Sir feels he needs to do. I know in my case as a boy, Master would always ask me my opinion, then he would either use it or tell me why he didn't use it and why he chose to do it his way which would usually taught me a thing or two about life, or what needed to be done. This process helped me to be educated in his way of thinking as well as to open the lines of my thoughts with him.

Some Masters/Sirs require diaries to be kept by a boy so as to be able to read their thoughts and feelings during each day to help understand their state of mind. My Master did this on an oral visitation with me each day so as we would openly discuss these issues and he would help me through this time to understand what needed to be done. Both are really quite good ways of communication between the two parties. I also kept a diary which held other things I couldn't speak of and he read that usually weekly and then discussed it with me. One is just silent and the other is totally open. It really depends on the Master/Sir and his thoughts on how he was to reach his submissive/boy. It does need to be stated that during this time anything the boy verbalizes or writes can have no repercussions or the boy will end up not telling the truth. These words written or verbalized are free from punishment no matter the content. This must be a hard and fast rule or it will fail.

In play, a boy's body was his Master/Sir's to use as he deemed necessary or to whatever level of play the Master/Sir had achieved. Since Master was a Council Member he was a well rounded educated dominate and I never knew what to expect in play. This made it more exciting sexually for me, as I never knew what to expect. It also made me more experienced as a bottom for I had to anticipate anything from him. This can be a good thing and more exciting but it also can be very frightening if the boy/submissive is not secure in who he is and or what he can handle in pain. It could also mean he might have to endure more than he normally would handle if he submitted to a known Master. But a good Master would be able to determine this boy/boi/submissive/slave level of play if the boy/boi/submissive/slave's body would speak to the Master, therefore allowing the Master to play to that level which was the Master/Sir obligation and duty.

In "Old Guard" days as well as with Master there were no limits. It was deemed that through your training, you should learn how to read a boy/boi/submissive/slave's body. A good Master/Sir should be able to make a boy/boi/submissive/slave submit and endure whatever the Master/Sir wanted if he knew how to manipulate and power exchange with that boy. If a boy/boi/submissive/slave had to have the scene stopped, it was said that the Sir or Master had not accomplished his techniques and should be stripped of his title and made to go back and relearn his techniques and title. It was considered that he didn't respect the leatherman's code which he had to have sworn to sometime during his mentorship. It was looked at as he had broken the trust which was agreed upon between the Master/Sir and boy/boi/submissive/slave and that was to determine that level through the body language. He was able to push the limits but not cause any permanent damage. If the boy/boi/submissive/slave just had stopped the scene because he didn't like it, that pressure was then put on the boy/boi/submissive/slave not to understand that he was to endure what the Master/Sir could give providing that the Master/Sir didn't cause permanent harm or cross any boundaries predetermined not to cross. This again became very subjective and questionable as times changed so this was put to the side when safe words were created.

Today, we have to have safe words due to the fact that many people do not know how to read the boy/boi/submissive/slave's body and therefore overplay the boy/submissive or hurt the boy/submissive. It can also be because the Master/Sir doesn't know what he is doing either with the tools of the trade. Therefore, when the computer age came into being and many people were getting hurt, the Safe Word came into existence to protect the boy/boi/submissive/slave/bottom. It gave the control back to the boy which really took away the real submission; now power exchange is looked at very differently than in "Old Guard" days. The power exchange was controlled by the Master/Sir not the boy.

A Master/Sir should be able to read his boy's body in play, if he is to be a great dominant. Body Language is something a boy should give out regularly and hopefully a boy will let it happen. Many a night I wondered if I would survive the play, knowing I had no say in what he did to me. I remember one night right after my approval by the council where he allowed all 15 men to use me in play. I thought this night I was going to die. My body was sore and bleeding. I was filled with many men's cum and I still had to be used finally by Master one final time. He also was the first to use me that night. Just as he began to use me for the last time, he walked up behind me and asked me how I was doing. I responded to him, I was scared. He whispered into my ear; "remember, I am a medical doctor. Nothing will happen here that I can't save you from." Those words brought me comfort believe it or not as I endured the balance of that evening. As one can see, trust here was critical and this is something every boy needs to have with his Master/Sir. Trust however must be earned as well as given by both parties. I trusted Master explicitly.

In "Old Guard" ways, a boy was always kept 24/7/365. He was collared with a simple chain around his neck for a short time, he wore the consideration collar. This was considered like the dating period. Next came the training collar, which was worn for the training period and was locked with a lock. Once he was trained and achieved all of his Master/Sir's needs during a training period, he was then given a permanent collaring ceremony, which again will be covered in the ceremony section of this book. The consideration collar was usually given just in front of the Master/Sir's immediate friends or family, no council needed to be present however could be. The training collar and permanent collar was always done with at least some of the council if not all of the council present as well as the community and family. In all instances in "Old Guard" the key was kept by the Master/Sir and never given to the boy or anyone else to keep.

Today boys don't always stay 24/7/365 with their Masters/Sirs and therefore the key is sometimes kept by the boy for travel reasons and other reasons such as work. This to me is a violation of the protocol of being a permanent collared boy but again this is my opinion only, because of my training and history. I do understand it however, and the reason necessary to do it this way.

A boy should earn his keep through outside work and share in the expenses of his life. I, however was not allowed to do this. I really did feel it made me more dependent on my Master, which wasn't an issue for him but became an issue for me. I didn't like not having money in my pocket that was mine and earned by me. It's something that can go either way and has to be discussed by the Master/Sir with his boy during the consideration collar so as not to cause a problem further down during his training and permanent collaring.

A boy also has the right to speak to other people in open conversation usually with the permission of his Master/Sir. Boy's may take open liberties with other boys in their own group and have open conversation with them as they are considered brothers in leather life. Boys however, should not speak to slaves in open conversation in high protocol as slaves should only be spoken to by their owner. Boy/boi/submissive could speak to slaves during social and low protocols. This again was depending on whether or not the slave was from the same family as the boy then this rule changed during high protocol as well as a boy could speak to his owner's slave as part of the family.

Outsiders and other Masters/Sirs should always ask permission to touch another boy from a Master/Sir. This also goes for kissing another person's boy. It's a common courtesy as well as it shows respect for the household of that Master/Sir. Even a Master should show respect to another Sir and ask for permission to touch or kiss another Sir's boy. Even though the Master has a higher level of status in the community, he still needs to be respectful of the rules of the community and the households. If a boy however reaches and does things on his own toward a Master or Sir, the Master or Sir can either look at the other Master/Sir and allow the action to happen or stop the action and ask if he has gotten permission. This really depends on whether the Master/Sir being greeted by the boy is well known to the Master/Sir's family.

In the event of a Master or Sir's death, the council or a council member would remove the boy's collar and that collar was destroyed. The lock must was also destroyed by fire or by smashing it with a sledgehammer. The collar belongs to the Master/Sir as does the lock and will always be with the Master/Sir. A boy was not to keep his collar in his Master's/Sir's memory. Again this is "Old Guard" Tradition.

Today many people keep all their collars. This would have been a taboo in "Old Guard" days. Once a Master/Sir has left the boy no trace of that Master/Sir's attachment to that boy is to be kept. In fact in some groups there is a rule that once a Master/Sir has passed, the boy is never to mention his name again. Only the council members may speak of that Master/Sir's name. The reason for this rule was to protect their name in years past and his involvement in the community.

Today, this is one of the rules which I can't support although my collar was removed and the lock smashed and the keys were put in my Master's coffin, I can't help but speak of him and I don't know how anyone could not want to speak of their Master/Sir after death as he was so important to my being and made me who I am today. I do not usually mention his name nor do I ever speak his last name. I always call him just Master. I have however, said just his first name a few times lately in reference to this book and the books I am writing to honor his name. You will never hear me speak his last name however in public. One never knows who is listening. He was from the time when things were kept private for his and my protection and I will honor that until I die.

Now, I have to say there are two types of boys as well: Alpha boy, known also as a senior boy in some relationships and Beta boy, known also as the junior boy. There can also be many other boys if the Master/Sir has a whole compound of boys. These boys would report to beta who in turn would report to alpha showing the due respect of each boy in the household. Much like the privates would report to the corporal and he would report to the sergeant and captain etc.

Alpha boy/senior boy is someone who has been trained by the Master/Sir and shows leadership abilities. It is only done when there are multiple boys in the Master/Sirs's care. Being in alpha position denotes the boy usually is very proficient in play, managing the household as well as the Master/Sir's affairs. He is the one the other boys of the household will go to for advice or guidance as well as the Master/Sir counts on to do and make the decisions regarding the family as a whole under the Master/Sir's guidance. In my eyes, he is like the Major Domo of a mansion or large household. An alpha boy is usually being groomed to become a Sir if he shows these tendencies and qualities.

Beta boy/Junior boy is the other boy in a triad relationship or second boy in command in a house of many boys. As the beta boy in a large household, he is the one whom the other boys would go to who in turn the beta boy would then go to the Alpha boy and get the final decision. In a two-boy house he is the second boy but in large families of boys this position really is the assistant to the alpha boy position in the household.

slave

The title of slave, much like that of the boy, is a submissive bottom recognized by the council. However, there are major differences between the two. The biggest difference is that a slave has no say in what the Master requests. Slaves always have a negotiated contract that is signed at the time of ownership stipulating all the terms of that Master/slave relationship. The slave's aim is solely to serve his Master. The slave agrees to surrender himself as well as all of his belongings, property and earnings to his Master. He must do as the Master orders with no reservations and with no rights to express himself unless given permission. This was "Old Guard "tradition. Today of course all this is negotiated in a slave contract as many slaves make more money than their Master.

Masters were the only ones who could own a slave. In "Old Guard" days it was thought that a Sir or anyone else was not responsible enough to actually own someone. It is for that main reason that many times even today you only see the words Master and slave together as this was just the way it was. Even in the contests, you even only see Master and slave words used never Master/Sir and slave. A slave however can refer to his Master as "Sir".

He surrenders his body as well to his Master to do as the Master wishes and with whomever the Master wishes. It is truly an ownership position of property and with that understanding the submissive must obey and do as he is told. Usually a slave stands at the side of the Master but at least one or two steps behind him. It is this distinction that publicly anyone should be able to recognize a boy from a slave. He generally remains speechless and stands at attention with head bowed or at parade rest, awaiting or anticipating the orders or needs of his Master.

A slave was generally known to give up reference to himself by name and call himself an it. In doing this, "Old Guard" felt that the word "it" would also help keep the slave in its proper head space and place. He would not be recognized by his name but it would refer to the Master's property.

A slave was generally never allowed to verbalize in a public setting, unless another Master/Sir spoke to him with his owner's permission. Most of these protocols are discussed during the introduction/negotiation time of ownership and prior to the signature of the contract by the slave. Once the slave contract is signed the only one who can break that contract is the Master.

A slave can ask the Master for the contract to be revoked but if the Master doesn't want to end it, the slave must abide by his signature and fulfill the terms of the contract. If the slave broke the contract and walked out on the Master/Sir, the slave would generally not be allowed back into the local leather community. In "Old Guard" households the slave was generally kept naked and in chains during service in the house. Only if non-leather company was to be received would the slave be allowed to be attired and chains removed.

A slave is then property of that Master until such time that the Master desires to rid himself of that slave and he is then sold or given off to another Master. Upon a Master death the slave is given to the council to be sold or given to another Master for his use. A slave is never, from the point of being entered into slavery by the council, allowed to determine his future. Today this would not be an acceptable way.

He is totally at the owner's discretion and use. A boy/boi/submissive is a volunteer; a slave is not a volunteer. Many men really enjoy this as they are very passionate and love giving up total control of their life in service to a superior Master. Remember, surrender and service are the key words in a slave's life.

A Master can have a household of many slaves and again the alpha/senior or beta/junior slave would apply. Much like that of the alpha and beta boy their responsibilities to the Master would be the same. The only difference between the boy and the slave is what has been stated above.

A Master can have also a boy or many boys as well as a slave or many slaves or any combination thereof. Here again the alpha position would need to be chosen by the Master and there can only be one Alpha and one Beta to a household. In this situation the Master has to make known who is who.

BOTTOM

The term bottom was the term used both in gay life and in leather life; it denoted the fact that you liked to be fucked or to be the person receiving the fuck. Many people think it wasn't part of the leather journey but leather men used it to refer to men who like to be fucked and receive their power exchanges. But in true "Old Guard" it was just that of being a fuck bottom or a oral sex giver. They were bottoms who enjoyed being fucked by a Top's/Dominant's/Daddy's/Sir's or Master's. They just like to be fucked and played with. Not that there is anything wrong with this but it was looked at in "Old Guard" as they were not serious play men but men who just enjoyed sex with no power exchange.

Bottom in a pansexual world is simply someone who enjoys being the receiver in play with no sexual overtones and no service, as Top is strictly the administrator of the play with no expectations of either. In pansexual terminology there are girls, boy/boi (s), daddy's girl (s), mommy's girl/boy, daddy's girl/boy, mommies, daddies, little's, baby girl/boy, pony, trainers, and it goes on and on. These are more fetish roles but I will defer to the pansexual group to define all these as they are really far more definitive and out there than our gay male leather rolls. They are not always involving leather attire nor are they part of "Old Guard".

TRAINING OF A BOY IN "OLD GUARD" LIFESTYLES

Once a boy has been selected to be owned property and accepts his collar, now comes the daunting task of beginning his training. If a boy is serious and willing to go into service to one Master you have to be make clear for all parties the details of that collaring, the meaning as well as what training that is to be expected. First, you have to be sure he is willing to make the commitment to you and not to allow others to interfere in his training. In "Old Guard" life it was much easier, today, because simply there weren't many people available out there to train someone. Today many people feel they can train someone but no one person will train the same with the same information. This is why I am writing this book to help Master/Sirs lay down a format in which they can achieve a successful trained boy. Many Master/Sirs never really know what and how to train someone so let me give you some basics to follow that were used on me in my training.

First off I had to sign a commitment letter stating that I was only going to receive training from one Master/Sir. If other training was given to me by other people I would bring it and present that training so that my Master/Sir could approve it and take it into his training of me. Many times I would receive information from people in the bar and my Master would say to me you will learn that in time but let it go for now for it is not important and we will revisit it when we reach that time. I would then try to do so.

As the first real step after signing the letter of commitment, I was given the positions in protocol. I was given a period of time to learn them and daily, I would be asked several times to assume the position of day. Then after the first day I would then be asked to assume two different positions on day two, third day I would be tested on three positions and so on until Master would give a command and I would then assume that position. This generally took about one month.

After the positions were achieved on command I was then given hand signals to learn. This would take approximately 2-3 weeks in which the hand signals and positions were drilled into my head to become properly trained as to how and under what circumstance I would take a position by hand signals.

Once the positions and hand signals were learned, the types of protocol followed. I had to understand what was involved in each protocol and when the three types of protocol would and could be used. Again this usually took about one month for each type of protocol. I understand some people learn faster than others, so all of these timetables are truly estimates and can be changed depending on the individual boy/boi/submissive/slave. This was harder than it sounds and many times Master would just say tonight will be in low protocol or high protocol and I would then know what to expect. I sometimes found it harder to understand which protocol to use until I learned all the types of protocol and when usually they were used.

Next was how to address the various levels of hierarchy. Here there seems to be great opportunities as the community nowadays is much larger and not regimented or disciplined so we know who is who and how they should be addressed. If a boy does know if a Master/Sir is present what would be said and how he would act. Many people tend to ask questions about it. After they have seen the protocol performed publicly they begin to learn and understand it. A prime example happened the other night. I had my boy next to me and a man joined our conversation after appropriately asking permission to join us. I, as a Master, in this community, had no knowledge of who he was so I extended my hand and he introduced himself as Tom.

I had no idea by the way he dressed as to who or what he was. So I introduced my boy to him saying, "Tom this is my collared boy and boy this is Tom". Not until later in the conversation did he reveal he was a Sir. Now here is where it gets hard for me as an "Old Guard" leatherman. I did not know him as a Sir nor did I know if he should get that respect of "Old Guard". But when in doubt I had to go with his title and assume he knew what he was talking about until his true colors showed. My boy showed him true respect in "Old Guard" ways regarding his title and stood on point awaiting further discussion with him and spoke only when spoken to. My boy acted appropriately here as he had been trained. He also asked for permission to relieve himself which I granted. Upon the boy's return I offered to buy Tom a beer. The boy realizing I had proposed a beer proceeded to the bar and retuned kneeling and presented me my beer saying "Sir your beer?" I then said "thank you boy". boy turned to Sir Tom and presented him his beer saying "your beer Sir" serving Sir Tom. He then stood and assumed the on point position holding his beer in front of him. This was a true example of good low protocol in a bar environment using correct terminology and protocol traditions.

After the hierarchy, the boy would learn the rules and protocol statements and put them to memory. He would be tested as to what was accepted in "Old Guard" protocol and what was not. The Master/Sir would propose daily situations or questions to test the rules of protocol until such time that all the rules and protocols would be answered correctly without any hesitation. This was repeated until such time as they became second nature to the boy/boi/submissive/slave. This again could be time consuming and really depending on the boy/boi/submissive/slave mental capabilities could this be achieved.

Also over the lifetime of the boy these rules and protocols were questioned, and any changes or updates noted and written down in the commitment contract so they can uphold a strict, sturdy environment for which both parties can educate and live by. The revisiting of these rules and protocols needs to be done at least once a year so as to update any changes that may have occurred. A good source to keep the record of the changes as they happened is the boy/boi/submissive/slave's diary on which his questions/comments and or changes could be noted. When the Master/Sir reviews these it makes a good time for open discussion to happen between the Master/Sir and his boy/boi/submissive/slave to talk about the change. Remember, that our lifestyle is changing constantly these days. I know in my case my boy and I have many conversations on what is changing and why we should change, either for acceptance among the leather community, the community at large or just because we simply don't have the need for this to be in our lives any longer. Remember, when you sign the letter of commitment each of the rules and protocols need to be adhered to so as each party

understand what they are getting into and reviewed periodically. This commitment letter makes for life to be so much simpler and easy to abide by.

Behavior in Public

Standing – any time the boy/boi/submissive/slave was in public with his Master/Sir, the boy would assume the **Public Present** – that was, the boy would maintain **Public Present** position slightly behind the Master/Sir's right shoulder(if right hand dominant), head bowed slightly but with full vision of his Master/Sir.

- If the Master/Sir was in a low protocol event or leather event where they understood protocol

the boy/boi/submissive/slave would always assume the **On Point** position again standing slightly behind the right shoulder of the Master/Sir. This would also denote to the other people in the event that this boy/boi/submissive/slave was in service to this Master/Sir as to the location of the boy/boi/submissive/Slave stance and position.

So long as the Master/Sir was standing, the boy would remain standing in that physical location. If Master/Sir wished to come around to a position facing him, he would either instruct the boy/boi/submissive/slave to move into his range of vision or used the families silent hand signals to cause the boy/boi/submissive/slave to change positions.

A slave position would be the same with more head bowed forward but with his Master/Sirs vision in full view using peripheral vision and a one full step back.

Initial meeting with a Leather Master, not a Sir

The boy would treat a Leather Master with the highest protocol respect, the same respect and deference that the boy showed his Master/Sir.

The boy would never speak to a Leather Master without specific permission or without prior instruction. When being introduced to a Leather Master, the boy would assume a **Standing Present** position, eyes and head slightly lowered. The boy would not extend his hand or provide any gesture of personal recognition, however, the boy would step out and bow and then resume the default position one step behind and to the right of his Master/Sir in a **Standing Present** position.

If his Master/Sir decided to introduce any Master to the boy, the boy would respond to the introduction and raised his eyes slightly thus: "Master ABC, this boy is honored and privileged to meet you, Sir." By stating the Master's name it gave any other boys a clue that there was a Master in the room so they could be properly introduced or show the proper respect. It was funny how when boys/bois/submissive/slaves would change their attitude in "Old Guard" days when a Master's name was mentioned. It was almost like flypaper to flies. If it wasn't for the sex they might have, it was for just being known and introduced to a real Master. It also meant they stood the chance they may be played with or eventually owned by him. In "Old Guard" days, boys felt the privilege of being owned by a Master more than by a Sir. It was all about the prestige it may bring them by being so owned. boy/ boi/submissive/slave's need to remember that ownership is a privilege and an honor and a gift. Don't abuse that collar. Cherish it and own up to your privileges and honors for that collar. You will be respected more and earn more respect by how you handle yourself in any given situation with a collar worn and proper attitude.

Key Commentary (among Sirs):

When two Leathermen meet, the Leatherman of highest rank would extend his hand first to the Junior. Often, there was a pregnant moment while the two Leathermen sort out who is senior. Masters were and still are always above a Sir. The Master would always state his name first and await the remaining Sir's name. Most people don't know this protocol and many people just introduce friends but whether attending a formal leather event or social or just in a bar environment true "Old Guard" men would respond highly to this protocol and feel very special by acknowledging their years and experience through leather. Always include their title. If there are multiple Masters involved it would go by senior to junior years of age. I as an "Old Guard" Leatherman know instantly if someone has "Old Guard" training based upon this protocol. It is a true key to knowing ones teaching by this protocol.

Key Commentary (other Sirs and boy):

One of the most disrespected things a boy could do when greeting a Leatherman – whether or not a Leather Master – was to smile broadly and offer a hand shake. The proper introduction of a boy would be: from Sir to another Leather Master/Sir. Always introducing any Masters first.

"Master/Sir ABC, I would like to introduce you to my boy, bill"

"boy bill, this is Master/Sir ABC"

boy could respond after the introduction by saying " Master/Sir ABC it is indeed an honor and a privilege to meet you Master/Sir."

boy's/boi's/submissive's/slave's could also introduce two unknown Master/Sir's to one another by properly saying.

"Master/Sir ABC it give me great honor and respect to introduce you to Master/Sir DEF" and then repeat "Master/Sir DEF and a great honor and respect to introduce you to Master/Sir ABC". Remember here to always introduce the Master first should one be present. Then again do senior to junior in chronological age within the title.

The boy/boi/submissive/slave would then be silent for the introduced Master/Sir's to exchange their own greetings. If it was a Sir that was being introduced to a Master, the Sir would wait for the handshake to be extended and any words to be spoke in their exchange as a matter of protocol. If two Masters were introduced either one could start the exchange usually though the senior age one should begin the conversation. Once the exchange started it was proper for the boy/boi/submissive/slave to step away allowing the Master's/Sir's to get to know one another. If the boy/boi/submissive/slave was needed he would either be asked to join them in the conversation or it would be stated to the boy "there is no need for you to leave boy, you may join us in conversation". At that point he would remain on point position and wait to be spoken to by either party and then respond.

Physical proximity when others are present:

If the boy's Master/Sir was in private discussions with another Master, the boy would remove himself from within ears hearing, but remain within eye contact of his Master/Sir. If the boy was approached by someone else during this time, the boy would inform that person politely that he is not free to speak, that the boy is attending his Master/Sir but the Master/Sir is in private conversation. This is usually done only in low and high protocols. The boy should remember in social protocol if this situation is occurring to try to give the Master/Sir's the same respect without being so overt.

- The boy would not leave the point position of attending without instruction or permission to do so. This was done with hand or verbal commands and a boy should never feel cheated of conversation when asked to do so. The boy/boi/submissive/slave would be told of the conversation when and if the Master/Sir felt it needed to be shared with the boy/boi/submissive/slave at a later point.

- In other instances, the boy would maintain correct on point position. In some tribes on **Point Position** was known as **Healing position**.

Although this may seem overly strict, these behaviors were and are necessary when other leather people were and are present and should be done today. In my opinion, today many things are just openly said. They should not be open to everyone's commentary. It somehow loses its importance and structure that was so predominate in "Old Guard" ways. All this was done so that the boy/boi/submissive/slave would be attentive to his Master/Sir and in so attentiveness the Master/Sir would communicate at any time with his boy/boi/submissive/slave telling him what he needed to know or what was discussed and with the appropriate commentary. This way it kept the Master/Sir views private to the boy/boi/submissive/slave without the boy being involved or influenced by someone other than his Master/Sir. Today much drama and miscommunication could be avoided if this were followed.

Socializing in Public:

Leathermen would understand the protocols and symbols and would respect the boy's position within the family. Similarly, the boy would recognize and respect protocols and symbols from other Leather families if involved at other family's events or homes. However, the visiting boy must be informed of these protocols should any be used.

Under no circumstances would a boy touch a Leatherman without specific permission. This was a serious sign of disrespect. In the presence of Leathermen, Masters/Sirs would be awarded the respect of their positions. The boy would refer to them by the honorific title by which they were introduced and afforded the courtesy given to Masters/Sirs. Boys would always address all the Master's first then the Sir's followed by the Daddies when in large groups showing proper respect and protocol. This can be difficult at times, but if you get it right it's a feather in your cap as a well-trained boy.

It was not appropriate to converse with other boys while in active service to a Master/Sir or if a scene is taking place.

In the event that a Leatherman endeavors to hug a boy, but this person has not negotiated with his Master/Sir for permission, the boy would accept the hug – but not return the hug – with grace and tact. The boy would be careful to avoid publicly embarrassing the Leatherman. Let me make this very clear. If the leatherman was a family member or some local friend this could be an exception however, in general, leathermen don't touch other leathermen without previous introduction or friendships that exists and from those friendships hugs, kisses, etc. can all be determined as normal practice. It is only when the leatherman is not part of the family nor known to the leatherman that this is the total proper behavior.

If this situation occurs out of his Master/Sir's sight, or occurs a second time, the boy would inform the novice Leatherman that he was in protocol and, with respect, did not have permission to return the hug. The boy would stand still during this exchange, but then leave the area promptly to report the incident to his Master/Sir. His Master/Sir then should return to the individual and explain the protocol.

When attending an event in High Protocol the boy would not use furniture, unless specifically directed to do so. He would attend his Master/Sir's side at all-times unless otherwise told to do so, remembering a few things.

1. The boy/boi/submissive/slave's head should never be higher than his Master/Sir's. Again this can be difficult if the boy is taller than the Master/Sir.

2. The boy/boi/submissive/slave should remain standing as long as his Master/Sir is standing and sit on the floor when the Master/Sir sits and otherwise directed.

3. The boy/boi/submissive/slave should attend to all his Master/Sir's needs acknowledging his Master/Sir's commands with a nod of the head.

4. The boy/boi/submissive/slave should always use all titles when addressing anyone.

5. The boy/boi/submissive/slave should remain silent unless spoken to.

If boys only were present and they were amongst their own boys group, they were allowed to talk freely amongst themselves about their lives, but would never reveal private and personal information about their Master/Sir nor any boy/boi/submissive/slave to another boy of their group. Only positive energy would be spoken about any Master/Sir in a community or unless the boys knew of unsafe play or some other reason where a Master/Sir would be spoken about to other boys for their safety. All other negative talk would be deferred to their Master/Sir for discussion. In "Old Guard", a Master/Sir's name was never talked about negatively amongst boy/boi/submissive/slave's. If a Master/Sir had an issue amongst the community it was up to the other Master/Sir's to handle the issue not the boy/boi/submissive/slaves.

If a boy knew of someone who was unsafe and was not holding up the protocols of the community and or was injuring people by our creed, they would immediately report it to their Master/Sir. Their Master/Sir would defer this to the Council. The Council decided as to how things would be handled. Whoever this person was, it needed to be dealt with immediately. This way no one was hurt further. This was not a discussion for the boys to have but one only for the boys to reveal and only to their Master/Sir. The boys' statements would be held in confidence. Remembering the words of our seniors, our words are the bonds that make the groups who they were. We took oaths as Master's/Sir's to protect the boys/bois/submissives/slaves and in that they trust.

CEREMONIES

Now let's talk about a few of the ceremonies which were so alive back in the days of "Old Guard". I hope you will understand that these were truly how we celebrated our achievements. A ceremony was a wonderful celebration celebrating an achievement. Here I am telling the ceremonies as I practice them today, some of the things I have added such as the HIV section to these ceremonies, as in "Old Guard" Times it wasn't an issues. I am asked almost daily for one of these ceremonies to be sent somewhere. Please note these only are the formats in which they were written and are still today being written with a few minor changes. They can be altered and were altered to fit the men of the times, and now genders would have to possibly be changed, but the meanings are still there. We did add music to some of these as some of the men were music lovers and wanted it and some didn't want the wax or blood and/or piss but wanted more symbols of what they were efficient at and made more sense for their immediate families. Because blood is so subjective today, for obvious reasons, anything could be replacing it but it should be something of great meaning to the parties involved. Today, not only a collar but celebration rings are used in some instances. Just remember, in "Old Guard" tradition and rituals leathermen were not about jewelry. I believe though, to each his own when it comes to celebrations. Make them as grand and as ritualistic as possible to have some meaning to all the parties it involves.

I recently had the great pleasure of covering the current IML 2009, Jeffrey Alan Payne. It had been mentioned to me that he has done so much for our community and being a good friend of his, as well as a mentor in his play, I was asked to personally cover him in "Old Guard" tradition by some "Old Guard" friends. His cover ceremony verbatim is here written. I hope not only for history but for traditional value to each of you, this will hold meaning as well as be documented for all of us to enjoy and remember this man, as he truly has done so much for our community in his title year worldwide. If you don't know him, I would highly recommend you get to know this incredible man and for all of you who do, I am sure you will agree with me. And to all of his friends, family and leatherfolk who were present that weekend at his home, we will remember this day with fondness, as a great day in his and our lives. It was truly a great honor to do this for him.

A COVER CEREMONY

Here was Jeffrey's public cover ceremony. It was done at his home just prior to his step down speech from being Mr. Texas. There were several members of the Boo Family (a leather family of Jeffrey Payne and David Roy, Jeffrey's husband) present and other leather friends from the community and his fellow title holders present and residing.

TO ALL GATHERED HERE let me introduce our brother Jeffrey Alan Payne and will he come forth and kneel before us here.

(Jeffrey enters and kneels before the three administering the ceremony.)

We are here today, leather family, for the purpose or recognizing one of our own and to give him the special honor that he has earned. We are going to officially cover Jeffrey Alan Payne, our leather brother and leader of greatness in our world leather community and here amongst his family and friends.

I am joined today to assist in this covering by David Roy, not only Jeffrey's Life partner and husband, but the Chamberlain to the Local Dallas Leather Knights which is required whenever someone is covered to have someone of high standards amongst the local community and clubs help officiate with the Elder. It is also my privilege to also have Lamalani, IMsL 2009 here to help officiate her leather brother and title year partner. She also represents the female leather community at large. It is also my privilege to share this with all of you his leather family, and friends here this 30th day of January, 2010

First off let me speak about Jeffrey. Jeffrey is not only an accomplished playwright, a recent graduate of Texas A and M, an honorary member of the San Francisco Mayoral Council, a member of the Dallas Leather Knights and many other honorary titles he has come to own worldwide during his title year as International Mister Leather 2009. I have also been his mentor in "Old Guard" lifestyles and teaching him to become a real BDSM player during his title year as our world leader in leather.

Through his year he has attended many types of events from leather contests to leather runs/educational events and I have been personally training him at these events as we have traveled through the world on how to play in a dungeon. Jeffrey has been taught and I attest to his public proficiency in the following areas.

He has learned to use the following:

A single tail whip,

Electric play with the ET 312 and violet wand,

He learned how to do not only standard sounds, but vibrating and ribbed sounds.

He also has become proficient in bondage, and mummification.

As well as his favorite, watersports.

In "Old Guard" tradition in order to earn the title of Sir, he has to earn his cover. He must demonstrate his ability to read the boy/boi/submissive/slave and execute the play with all the safety requirements and technique needed to build trust within in this play from his submissive/boy/slave. He has certainly done his community service worldwide and has been committed to charity work and other acts of kindness aiding our fellow brothers in their HIV evaluations. I hereby have witness and decree by "Old Guard" standards that he has met these requirements as is now worthy of another title and that being of the title Sir.

Having heard this, is there anyone here who would not agree that Jeffrey Alan Payne hasn't done enough for our community and has performed his levels of play to not award him this title. If so please speak now or forever hold your peace.

(A moment of silence to allow any objections.)

With no objections, we then want to go forth with his covering. Jeffrey also needs to be recognized for his outstanding compassion for people in our community and his dedication to his title, his partner and family, his friends and to people with the HIV virus and their journeys and to his special charity "Hearing from the Heart" and his outstanding work for people who need hearing aids. Jeffrey Alan Payne we salute this dedication.

Jeffrey, with this new title of Sir, you here by agree to accept the responsibilities that go along with that title of being not only a mentor, which God knows you have been to many, but also someone who will carry on the torch of leather history and play, for the remainder of your journey. You will also agree to continue your leather education and in play and hopefully someday attain a Master's title which shall also be part of your great journey.

The title of Sir means that you will covet the leather tribes in your heart, promote only educated play and understand that if you see or hear of anyone not playing by the covenants and by laws of the leather community of R.A.C.K. and Safe, Sane and Consensual, as well as know that each of us walk to our own drummer, take issue with that person and correct and educate them to the community at hand. The title of Sir holds power and yet compassion for all who enter into our life and as a Sir you agree to take that responsibility seriously and for whatever you can do to further each and every one of them as your brother and sister.

Jeffrey, I personally attest to knowing you well enough to bestow and honor you with this title and in front of your family, friends, and piers here today it gives me great pleasure to award you this cover.

(Hold His Cover)

This cover, in "Old Guard" tradition, is the symbol of your title. Wear this cover with all the knowledge that you have been officially covered in "Old Guard" tradition with all the history, honor and privilege that is represented in this cover. If you so accept this cover you hereby agree to covet those traditions set forth. Jeffrey, my brother, do you accept these responsibilities?

(Jeffrey responded) I do.

I hereby decree that Jeffrey Alan Payne has accepted these traditions, privileges', and understands the honor that is about to be bestowed upon him.

I now cover you Sir Jeffrey Alan Payne, IML 2009 (place the cover upon his head).

Know also that having now accepted and covered, you must wear this cover at all formal leather affairs and whenever in public other than in a dungeon. Know that the brim should never be touched by you or anyone else and when the cover is to be removed it is removed with both hands at the side, lifting off your head and then placing it into proper storage. If in a public space, the cover, if removed, should be lifted by both hands and place to your left side under your left arm with the brim facing forward and the open part of the hat to your side. This will allow the cover to wrap your body and keep its proper shape. If someone presents you with your cover or you ever present your cover to anyone it must be open side down and presented to you as you could reach out with both hands and just place it up and on your head. That would mean the cover is always away from the body of the person presenting it until such time that you are to take the cover from them and which point the brim should be turned and placed ready for you to accept the cover and just place it upon your head. This cover must be destroyed by fire at any point where as it becomes mutilated or your title stripped. Do you understand these rules?

(Jeffrey responded) I do.

I, John Weal, Master and Elder here do hereby declare you officially covered as Sir Jeffrey Alan Payne, IML 2009

Leather family, friends and all here please help me welcome our New Sir, Sir Jeffrey Alan Payne by all saying aye.

(All respond) Aye!

Congratulations Sir Jeffrey Alan Payne, IML 2009. You may rise and greet your family and friends.

Normally, a cover would be given only to a Master in "Old Guard" tradition. Today many Sir's are being covered due to their dedication and service and the difference today in the way we make our Sirs and Masters. For this reason only anyone who knows of Jeffrey Payne would agree he has achieved greatness in our leather community and should only by right be wearing the symbol of greatness in our leather community, his cover. It was for this reason only why he was covered.

He lives in greatness to the leather community in which he serves even after his step down.

GAUNTLET CEREMONY

A gauntlet ceremony is where one of our brothers of the community becomes recognized by the community as a Sir and at the point of his understanding the power exchange play which differs from being a dominant top. In "Old Guard" tradition, the gauntlet represents the first thing earned publicly, as a Sir by the community on that journey in traditional "Old Guard".

TO ALL GATHERED HERE let me introduce our brother _____ and will he come forth and kneel before us here.

(The brother steps forward and kneels)

We are here today, leather family, for the purpose or recognizing one of our own and to give him the special honor that he has earned. We are going to officially do a gauntlet ceremony to _____, our leather brother in our leather community and here amongst his family and friends from this day forward be known as he has entered his journey to become a Sir. The gauntlet represents the start and support of the leather family on this journey. When the covered is earned, it will be the two pieces of leather that will resemble your journey as a power exchange dominant Master. From the family, this gauntlet represents the beginning of your journey and from this day forward you shall only wear the single gauntlet on your left arm. This is a representation of understanding power exchange as a dominant and it doesn't represent anything more than that of the start of your journey and the support and love of you leather family in your journey. It is to help you understand that as the power dominant you must begin to respect the power you have as a dominant and that with that power come responsibilities. Those responsibilities are playing with your bottom safe, sanely and in consensual play along with the responsibilities of being aware of the Risk Aware Consensual Kink or R.A.C.K. as part of our leather creed. It also is the start of your own march to the drummer you are marching to with regard to the start of that leather journey as a Sir with hope of being a covered Master and knowledgeable about play. If you understand all these things respond by saying I understand the responsibilities being herewith stowed upon my journey by this gauntlet.

(Repeated by person) I understand the responsibilities being herewith stowed upon my journey by this gauntlet.

I hereby ask for your left arm and with this gauntlet tied I have passed on to you the "Old Guard" traditions which must be upheld. You do understand that tradition and agree to pass on the traditions of "Old Guard" as you someday will pass on the other gauntlet of this pair as you take on your leather family as a symbol of your journey and tradition. Do you acknowledge and promise to uphold these traditions? Do you understand the other piece to this pair of gauntlets is to be passed on to one of your brothers in your leather family?

(Repeat) I solemnly promise to uphold these traditions.

(The gauntlet is presented and put on the left arm of the new Sir. After the first gauntlet is put on the second gauntlet is handed to him to preserve to pass on as stated.)

Rise and greet your leather family as they welcome you to your new status as a beginning Sir. You now have to begin your formalized training understanding that you have sworn to uphold and honor R.A.C.K., Safe, Sane and Consensual Play, the traditions being passed on to you with the passing of the gauntlet and to always protect the leather tribe and to educate as well as take issue with anyone not practicing these traditions and creeds, correct them and educate them in the ways of real leather life and our community at hand.

I, Elder name, hereby officially declare you gauntleted by (leather family name) leather family.

You may rise and take your position within the community now and greet your family. Begin your journey as Sir _____!

COLLARING CEREMONIES

There were three types of collar ceremonies: a consideration collar, a training collar and a permanent collar.

A CONSIDERATION COLLAR CEREMONY:

A consideration collar ceremony was done when a Master/Sir found someone who he thought he may want to collar and call his own. This ceremony was usually privately done with very few people. Quite often just the Master/Sir and the boy/boi/submissive/slave were present. Others such as a close family member of someone well known to them could and would be present but no council member or public was there. He would place a simple chain around the boy's neck and lock it. He would tell the boy what this meant which basically meant he was now considered by the community to be off limits to anyone else but that Master/Sir. That this collar would be on for a designated time while they date making each other exclusive to each other and while the Master/Sir decides whether or not he is worthy of training. It was also a time when a boy/boi/submissive/slave would make the decision of whether or not he wanted to be exclusive with this Master/Sir. It was like the college pin or ring time with someone wanted you to go steady back in high school. Again be exclusive with one another. It was the first step then and it is the first step for a boy and a Master/Sir to take when they think they have found someone they want to be exclusive with. It was a time for each of them to get to know one another, their issues, their personalities, their lives. Much like what you would do back when you would go steady. Some basic training would be given to the boy but it wouldn't be as intense or as formalized as a training collar would be as it would be done in the presence of a council member and family and friends. They sometimes would move in together but it wasn't required as you were not in service to that Master/Sir 24/7/365. The boy would simply kneel in front of his Master/Sir and accept the collar. There may be some choice few words exchanged but there was no real formalized ceremony. The Master/Sir would simply explain what he wanted here and the boy/boi/submissive/slave would accept those words and discussion was had if any needed to be had. Many Masters/Sirs did this and never formally took the next step and their relationship went on for years. They would sort of let osmosis set in and the boy would learn bits and pieces through events and such but never formally receive training. For some this was good enough. For us "Old Guard" members this was only the beginning as we wanted to formally train our boy/boi/submissive/slave to properly wear the collar he had earned and give him the history and the training we expected in service to us men. The training collar was like boot camp was for the military. It was where they really received their training to go to battle. In "Old Guard" this step, a consideration collar, was only like signing the recruiting papers. You knew you were going to go to boot camp but you were simply getting yourself ready to be enlisted. The training collar meant you were enlisted and were at boot camp and doing your two year service time. The permanent collar was like you finished boot camp served some time and now you were signing up for a life time career in the military. I know most of you men can relate to all of these symbolisms as we either were part of this time or we have read about it.

A TRAINING COLLARING CEREMONY

All three collars are good for a boy/boi/submissive/slave. A consideration collar is usually done just between the parties and there the parties agree to begin to go into the one on one interaction with one another as a Master/Sir and a boy/boi/submissive/slave. It is usually done in the privacy of their own home or dungeon space. It generally is not a very public collaring. It is from that point that the parties can determine if they are compatible and determine what type of protocol that is going to be used. It is also during that time what traditions and rituals will be honored by the two. A time period is usually set for a short period on which all this is to be done so the training can commence and a training collar ceremony would be performed officially starting the public recognition of the said collar of the Master/Sir to the boy/boi/submissive/slave.

In January 2010, I met a great boy, boy travis. He had accepted a collar proposal by two wonderful men. They had given boy travis a consideration collar. I was asked by them to do their training collar ceremony to boy travis. I interviewed boy travis over a period of two days prior to agreeing to do their collaring ceremony. I also interviewed both the two men to understand why they wanted a boy in service to them as well as to understand their relationship and their commitment to leather educating this boy. After two days, I agreed to do their collaring. It was a great privilege for me again, for both leathermen, whom are friends. I having met them on numerous occasions prior, at Folsom Street and other events, prior to this weekend, which is why I was chosen to perform this ceremony. boy travis on the other hand was someone who not only had the looks of a boy but truly understood what it was to be a boy. I told them if they didn't collar him I would. boy travis was one of those wonderful boy/man who just exudes what it means to be a boy and wants and desires this life with all the joy and privilege it has. He understood what this life would be as becoming a trained boy and with that welcomed the opportunity with all his heart, open mind, and beautiful soul of that of a truly honest sincere boy. It was a big weekend for them as well as several other leatherfolk. That weekend had many highlights and this was one of the highlights of that wonderful weekend in Dallas. For the boy's/boi's/submissive's/slave's who were there, there were tears of joy in the room when the words were spoken. The women eyes present began to tear as well. The leathermen around the room stood quietly as you could see the look of incredible deep passion that dwelled in their hearts as these men taking their vows to each other in this training and the joy and hope for the future for the three of them. The room remained totally silent with camera's snapping as many had never witnessed such an event. Many had heard of this type of event but never witnessed it so they were not only excited about the event to happen but overwhelmed with feelings of what it all really meant. They were about to witness something that only they had heard about and to those leatherfolk, I am truly honored to be the one to have them present as this event happened.

To all of you who have witnessed an event such as this and understand all the meanings you will hopefully silently take these vows with them as we all did and know that in your hearts you honor their commitment should you ever meet them. I changed the word Master/Sir to his Sir's names as they were not officially Sirs at this time. I inserted boy travis into wherever the boys' name should be said. I was the elder. You will immediately read something very special. It will also show you how you can take this ceremony and make it your own by changing the names etc.

TO ALL GATHERED HERE, we are here for the purpose of an official training collar ceremony for (boy's name) soon to be known as boy (boy's name) collared to Master/Sir (the Master or Sir's name). This ceremony is something that the leather tribe looks upon as sacred, holy as well as a serious commitment. It is also known in "Old Guard" life that our word is our bond! It is intended for mentoring, nurturing, educating and loving as well as training our brother boy (name) into his life of service to Master/Sir (name).

I, (Elder's name), as the elder here officiating with (Full name and the position in the club or community as well as the name of the club, community, family) officiate this ceremony in behalf of these two men. (you can have as many official people from many organizations or communities here. The last collaring I did I had Sir Jeffrey Alan Payne, IML 2009, which I stated was the male side of our community as well as Lamalani, IMsL 2009 which represented the female side of our community, David Roy was the local club officiating member.) You all are here to bear witness to this collaring as the family, friends and leather tribe of these men. With all said how say you to this responsibility. If you agree you must say I agree.

(All respond) I agree.

Is there any known reason why this boy should not be collared today? If so please state the reason and who is objecting otherwise please remain silent.

(Slight pause for any person to speak)

With no response to the first call let us proceed to the second call. Who is sponsoring this boy for collaring and please bring him forth.

(At this time the boy is brought forth and generally by someone well known to the boy speaks, at boy travis collaring a friend of the family was his sponsor) I, (full name, title if any and from what organization) sponsor this boy.

First are the responsibilities of the Master/Sir (should always be at least a Sir to collar or higher). (State the full name of the Master/Sir and the club or community he is from) do you solemnly swear to abide by the rules of "Old Guard" leather tribe understanding that your purpose as boy (name of boy) mentor(s) you are responsible for nurturing, guiding, educating as well as understand that the open lines of communication must always be here in order for this relationship with you to grow. You understand that the collar of this boy means that he is in service to you and you must be responsible not only for his well-being but be his protector, educator and mentor as he begins his leather journey. You understand that in this you play critical roles in his daily routines. You must agree to mentor him in a way that won't violate any of the leatherman's creeds. R.A.C.K., Safe Sane and Consensual and that each of us walk to our own drummer as he will? Your household must provide a safe environment for him to grow, learn, and develop his leather education. Should you need guidance or assistance in this training, you will reach out to your leather brothers and ask for help with the understanding it must fit within your guidelines of your household and this contract. You understand that being under your guidance also requires that you must not abuse your power over your boy to be that of destroying his mental state and not under any circumstance must you ever use physical violence or punishable abuse in his training. That financially and emotionally you will support this boy to the best of your ability. The collar you hold represents that any person here forward in the leather tribe must ask your permission to touch your boy or have any contact with you boy and without your expressed permission will not be allowed to do so. This is done to protect him under your time as your collared boy. You must agree to take this commitment as serious as any relationship under God and know that you must welcome him to your household with your open heart, mind and body to fulfill his journey as a boy in service to you. What say you?

(The Master/Sir responds) I do.

boy (name of boy), you understand the from this point forward if you accept this collar having heard their responsibilities agree before everyone here that you fully understand their responsibilities to you set for by him and agree to receive his responsibilities to you with an open heart body and mind. That you too will honor the open lines of communication set forth above by your Sir. That at any such time you do not allow him to do his mentoring and educating as well as developing your growth as a leather boy in the community, that it is a direction violation of your duties in accepting this collar. The violation of not honoring that collar with your heart, mind, body, and soul you do realize at that point your collar would be removed and the lock destroyed. The punishment of being released from your duties and responsibilities of your collar would be the end result. You would then have to move out of his home and all educating and mentorship would cease.

You must also agree in so taking of this collar, it is the first step in your true "Old Guard" leather journey that will also help out in community service and do all that you possibly can do with the other local leather boys in service to help each other in times of need and service. That you will serve your Sir with all your heart, mind, body, and soul giving all that you can to achieve what you understand to now be your responsibilities as his collared boy. You also agree that you are going to relocate to become a 24/7/365 collared boy under his household and live in his household maintaining his household as soon as feasibly possible.

You understand that as his collared boy you do have the right to openly ask any questions on any order given but once you understand the directive completely you will be expected to follow that order as quickly as possible and as effectively as you bodily can. You also agree to accept the mentoring, guidance, and education as he set forth in his household and abide by all the rules of the household surrendering yourself physically as the promise to fulfill these requirements. That you will accept punishment when explained what error you made and never use profanity when addressing your Sir. You also hereby agree, upon relocating, you will actively pursue employment to help aid in the financial keeping of yourself as well as to contribute to the general household finances. You further agree to continue your academic education until such time you achieve the goals set forth by your Master/Sir and self and will be responsible financially to Master/Sir (Master's/Sir's name) for this privilege. You also agree to further your leather education and personal growth as his leather boy doing both community service and being in personal service to your Master/Sir.

boy (name), you do understand that all this is said and done under "Old Guard" rules and traditions and that understand that it is not only an honor but a privileged to be in service to Sir (Sirs name).

If you understand all what I have said and agree to it what say you.

(Boy responds) I do.

You now understand that by agreeing here you will be known as boy (boy's name) and that you do all this with your own sound mind and free will? If you agree and understand say, I do.

(Boy responds) I do.

You do this without any reservations knowing that this training collar represents a period of (state length of time and dates) If you agree and understand say, I do.

(Boy responds) I do.

Sir (his name) and boy (his name) understand that on or before the (dates mentioned above) a date must be discussed to enter into a permanent collar or further training collar must be discussed and decided on or boy (name) 's release of his collar and his position along with all the stipulations in this contract become null and void. If you both agree and understand say, I do.

(Master/Sir and boy responds) I do.

It is also understood that boy(name) will keep a written daily journal of his education, feelings, emotions and mentoring so when and if asked by his mentor or members of the council that any of these people will understand where the boy is, his feeling and what may be needed to further his development of service. boy (name) understands he is free to write freely all of his feelings, concerns, or thoughts knowing that anything written in this journal is considered sacred and no repercussion of any sort can be done to him from his writings. If you understand this statement you must respond, I do.

(Master/Sir and boy respond) I do.

(This next part can be private or public depending on the Sir and the boy's feeling)

Boy (name) you are knowledgeable of as of this date to the HIV status and health conditions of Master/Sir (Sir's name). You also are aware of your HIV Status and health conditions and have shown Master/Sir (Sir's name) yours. You both swear to practice sex as safely as possible unless otherwise negotiated and if negotiated not to, understand that you are entering into this relationship with the possibility of further infection to each of you. You hereby are actively involved with each other and understand the risks of all sexually transmitted diseases are your responsibilities and shall have no recourse unless otherwise stated here should an infection occur along your journey. You also have agreed upon to the sexual freedom and boundaries established prior to this date and agree to abide by these during the period stated in this contract. You both do this freely and with sound mind and affix your initials below knowing the possible repercussions which may result if you open the relationship and understand there is no recourse if the contracted is altered. This contract includes the exchange of all fluids including but not exclusive to blood, piss and cum.

(Write and initial the initials of the parties)

(Back to public)

> In the unforeseen event of the death of Master/Sir (Master's/Sir's name) or in the event you decide to revoke this contract, the collar must be removed. In revoking the contract or ending this contract the lock must be smashed and then put into flames for its destruction and a new collar and lock should be used if the boy be further collared? A new contract must be executed to any new Master/Sir or any timetable in accordance with "Old Guard" tradition to all parties.
>
> Now in keeping of the honor of "Old Guard" tradition, Master/Sir (Master's/Sir's name) please light your candle. The candle fire represents the light of the future of this boy. May you never stifle or snuff this light as you Master/Sir (Master's/Sir's name) are responsible for his growth, education and training of boy (boy's name) not only in leather life but in non-leather life. You also understand that by you dropping the wax down the back of your boy; you are hereby sealing your commitment to him on his body. The wax that drips down your body boy (boy's name) is his commitment to you and that he herby seals his promise to live up to his commitments to you, say I do.
>
> Boy (boy's name) by enduring this dripping, you understand that your body is the canvas on which this contract is being sealed. You agree to all the conditions and commitments set forth in this contract and will abide by them with your body, mind and soul accepting this dripping as your commitment back to him of your agreement to allow this honor and privilege to begin.
>
> If you both agree please answer I do.

(Both respond) I do.

> You may begin to drip the wax down your boys' back. The wax need to go from his shoulder to his waist signifying the sign of commitment by you here. The dripping wax area symbolism from his shoulders to his waist represents the back on which the boy will service his Master/Sir through his commitments and play.

(All parties officiating must drip the wax as the community representatives as well as the Master/Sir.)

> Next we move to the fluid exchange. You hereby agree to this exchange of fluids so you and your Master/Sir (insert Master/Sir's name) are fluid bonded setting the president that nothing shall be between you and your Master/Sir in service. You both lie down your lives for each other in this part of the ceremony. You both will seal this by drinking from this cup which will contain your fluids and the fluids set forth by this member of the council and clubs attending. This cup represents your commitment to each other, to your leather life with these organizations and to the leather family of which you now join. We all shall join in this declaring you fluid bonded with this family, each other, and your organizations of leather. Do you hereby agree to this? If you do say, I do.

(They both agree by saying I do individually. The Master/Sir goes first followed by the boy.) I do.

(The elder pisses into the cup followed by the attendees then topped by the Master/Sir and his boy/boi/submissive/slave symbolizing their commitment to each other and the community.) Today this can be varied by just the Master/Sir and the boy/boi/submissive/slave due to local issues with HIV and HEP c etc. (This part of the ceremony is highly recommended if they are going to not practice safe sex as a declaration to the family of their commitments which have to be discussed openly with the Elder prior to the ceremony.) Even though piss is classified the safest form of fluid exchange, it has to be openly discussed prior to the ceremony. I have also done this where blood is exchanged for piss mixing the blood by a simple prick of the fingers. (Again any symbolism can be added to this part of the ceremony. Just be sure it has proper symbolic reasons to the parties involved.)

> Everyone here is witnessed to this dripping and sealing of the commitment and agrees to uphold, cherish and guide this new leather family. Everyone here also agrees to honor the right and commitment of this leather family amongst yourselves and the community. To the

family, friends and leather tribe here today we all agree to bear witness to the growth of this boy and collar set forth today on his body. We all have agreed upon to accept this sealed commitment this date for the period set forth by this contract. If you agree may we all please say, I do.

(All respond) I do.

It gives me great honor and privilege to have Master/Sir (Sir's name) collar his boy (boy's name) this ___ day of (month and year). Please collar your boy and secure the lock.

(Boy is collared and locked)

Master/Sir (Sir's name) you are now the keeper of the key and only in extreme circumstances must the key be released. The circumstance in which the key and collar are to be removed are only for the well-being of the boy and he understands that the key may be given to him only during this time for the removal and reattachment while the well-being of his life is in question. Upon relocking the collar, the key must be returned to his Sir for safe keeping. The collar and lock must be worn at all times and never removed unless for the well-being of this boy only.

To all here I am proud to announce the collaring and commitment of Master/Sir(Sir's name) and boy (boy's name). May we all honor this commitment from this point forward not only in "Old Guard" tradition and protocol but to this family. You may all congratulate the newly collared boy (boy's name) to his Master/Sir (Sir's name).

This should be written or typed out. All officiating members as well as all the parties should sign including the sponsor. This contract should also be sure to have all dates clearly stated and should be revisited by all within the time span of the contract for furthering of the boy's life as well as any new contracts. Music and other things can be added to make for a larger more elaborate celebration.

A PERMANENT COLLAR CEREMONY

TO ALL GATHERED HERE, we are here for the purpose of an official permanent collar ceremony for (boy/slave's name) soon to be known as boy/slave (boy's name) collared to Master/Sir (the Master or Sir's name). This ceremony is something that the leather tribe looks upon as the highest commitment of a boy not only sacred, holy as well as a serious permanent commitment with no out. It is also known in "Old Guard" life that our word is our bond! It is intended for a lifetime commitment of service with no out doing only as the Master/Sir stipulates. It is also recognized that whatever property and belongings this boy/boi/ owns becomes that of his Master/Sir. This commitment also expects the boy/boi to live in Master/Sir's Household 24/7/365 and together for the rest of their lives build one life committed together in life, in leather and in love with all the respect, honor and tradition that "Old Guard" represents as well as the strictness, structure and stability which we uphold in our lives.

I, (Elder's name), as the elder here officiating with (Full name and the position in the club or community as well as the name of the club, community, family) officiate this ceremony in behalf of these two men. (You can have as many official people from many organizations or communities here.) You all are here to bear witness to this permanent collaring as the family, friends and leather tribe of these men. With all this said how say you to this serious commitment and responsibility. If you agree you must say I agree.

(They both respond) I agree.

Is there any known reason why this Master/Sir and boy/boi/submissive should not have the ability to have and hold a permanently collar today? If so please state the reason and who is objecting otherwise please remain silent.

(Slight pause for person to speak)

With no response to the first call, let us proceed to the second call. Who is sponsoring this boy/boi/submissive for permanent collaring and what family represents this Master/Sir and please bring them forth.

(At this time the Master/Sir boy/boi/submissive is brought forth. The sponsor is generally well known to the boy/slave. If he has a Daddy it would be him.

Usually the head of the family brings forth the Master/Sir or highest family member if it's the Master/Sir's family. Generally theses peoples will speak briefly of their sides and sponsorship of these two men with the Master/Sirs family speaking first.)

> I, (Elder/Master or head officiator full name) as well as all of you have heard from sponsors of this family member of this Master/Sir and the sponsors of this boy/boi/submissive. Do you believe they are ready for this permanent collaring? The Master/Sir has had his training and boy/boi/submissive has been properly trained under the training collar as well as he accepts the responsibilities of a lifetime of service and they both accept the responsibility to one another and understand what this commitment of permanent collar means to each other and in leather life. How say all of you? If you believe please answer I believe.

(Everyone else states) I believe.

> First are the responsibilities of the Master/Sir (should always be at least a Sir to permanently collar or higher). (State the full name of the Master/Sir and the club or community he is from) Do you solemnly swear to abide by the rules of "Old Guard" leather tribe understanding that your purpose as boy/boi (name of boy) owner (s), you are responsible for his well-being and mental state as well as understand that the open lines of communication must always be here in order for this relationship with you to grow. You understand that the permanent collar of this boy/boi means that he is in permanent service to you and you must be responsible not only for his well-being but be his protector, educator and owner as he continues his leather journey. You understand that in this you are solely responsible for his daily routines. You must agree in owning him in a way that won't violate any of the leatherman's' creeds. R.A.C.K., Safe Sane and Consensual and that each of us walk to our own drummer as he will? Your household must provide a safe environment for him to grow and serve you as well as further his leather life in service. Should you need guidance or assistance in this ownership, you will reach out to your leather brotherhood and ask for help with the understanding that it must fit within your guidelines of your household and this contract. You understand that being his owner, you also understand that you must not abuse your power over your boy to be that of destroying his mental state and not under any circumstance must you ever use physical violence or punishable abuse in his ownership. That financially and emotionally you will support this boy/boi/submissive to the best of your ability. The permanent collar you hold represents that any person

here forward in the leather tribe must ask your permission to touch your boy/boi/submissive or have any contact you're your boy and without your expressed permission will not be allowed to do so. This is done to protect him under your time as your permanent collared boy/boi/submissive. You must agree to take this commitment as serious as any relationship under God and know that you must welcome him to your household with your open heart, mind and body to fulfill his journey as a boy/boi/submissive in service to you for the remainder of your life and or his life. You promise to stand by him in sickness and in health for richer or poorer, and for whatever may happen during your lifetime of ownership? You promise to uphold the strictness, structure and stability that is necessary to keep your relationship alive and growing in the honor and respect of one another as well as "Old Guard" Tradition. You have trained and collared him under your ways and he is fully aware with no secrets as to your life? What say you?

(The Master/Sir responds) I do.

Boy/slave (name of boy), you understand the from this point forward if you accept this permanent collar having heard your owners responsibilities agree before everyone here that you fully understand these responsibilities set for by your Master/Sir and agree to receive these responsibilities and communicate openly with him. You must agree to take this commitment as serious as any relationship under God and know that you must welcome him to your life with your open heart, mind and body to fulfill your journey as a boy in service to him for the remainder of your and or his life. You promise to stand by him in sickness and in health for richer or poorer and for whatever may happen during your lifetime of ownership? You promise to uphold the strictness, structure and stability that is necessary to keep your relationship alive and growing in the honor and respect of one another as well as "Old Guard" Tradition and rituals. Master/Sir (his name) has temporarily trained and collared you under his ways and he is fully aware with no secrets as to your life? What say you?

(Boy responds) I do.

That you too will honor the open lines of communication set forth above by your Master/Sir. The violation of not honoring this collar with your heart, mind, body, and soul you do realize at that point your permanent collar would be removed and the lock destroyed. The punishment of this being considered a total violation of what you have promised here today and you would be released from your duties and responsibilities of your permanent collar. The end result would mean you would then have to move out of his home and all educating and mentorship would cease. You also understand that a violation of this sort would cast you out of this community as a breach of your word which is what honor we all stand upon? How say you.

(Boy responds) I do.

You must also agree in so taking of this collar, it is the last step in your true "Old Guard" leather journey as a boy that will also help out in community service and do all that you possibly can do with the other local leather boys in service to help each other in times of need and service. That you will serve your Master/Sir with all your heart, mind, body, and soul giving all that you can to achieve what you understand to now be your responsibilities as his Permanent collared boy. You also agree that you are going to relocate to become a 24/7/365 collared boy under his household and live in his household maintaining his household as soon as feasibly possible.

You understand that as his permanent collared boy you do have the right to openly ask any questions on any order given but once you understand the directive completely you will be expected to follow that order as quickly as possible and as effectively as you bodily can. You also agree to accept the continuation of his mentoring, guidance, and education as he set forth in his household and abide by all the rules of the household surrendering yourself physically as the promise to fulfill these requirements. That you will accept punishment when explained what error you made, should you make one, and never use profanity when addressing your Master/Sir. You also hereby agree upon relocating, you will actively pursue employment to help aid in the financial keeping of yourself as well as to contribute to the general household finances. You further agree to continue your academic education until such time you achieve the goals set forth by your Master/Sir and self and will be responsible financially to Master/Sir (Sir's name) for this privilege. You also agree to further your leather education and personal growth as his leather boy being in personal service to your Master/Sir.

boy (name), you do understand that all this is said and done under "Old Guard" rules, traditions and rituals and understand that it is not only an honor but a privileged to be in permanent service to Master/Sir (Sirs name).

If you understand all what I have said and agree to it what say you.

(Boy responds) I do.

> You now understand that by agreeing here you will be known as boy (boy's name) and that you do all this with your own sound mind and free will? You understand also that this is a permanent collar and must always be worn except if your life is in jeopardy. You understand that all other agreements during the training collar including the blood, fluid exchange, and sealing of the commitment still are to be upheld. If you agree and understand say, I do.

(Boy responds) I do.

> You do this without any reservations knowing that this permanent collar represents now the remainder of your life unless violated. If you agree and understand say, I do.

(Boy responds) I do.

> Master/Sir (his name) and boy (his name) understand that on this day for the rest of their lives on earth this collar must be honored. boy (name) 's release of his collar and his position along with all the stipulations in this contract become null and void only in death or violation of his Master/Sir (name). If you both agree and understand say I do.

(Master/Sir and boy responds) I do.

> It is also understood that boy(name) will continue to keep a written daily journal of his education, feelings, emotions and mentoring so when and if asked by his Master/Sir or members of the council that any of these people will understand where the boy is, his feeling and what may be needed to further his development of service. boy (name) understands he is free to write freely all of his feelings, concerns, or thoughts knowing that anything written in this journal is considered sacred and no repercussion of any sort can be done to him from his writings. If you understand this statement you must respond, I do.

(Master/Sir and boy respond) I do.

(This next part can be private or public depending on the Sir and the boy's feelings.)

Boy (name) you are knowledgeable of as of this date to the HIV status and health conditions of Master/Sir (Master/Sir's name). You also are aware of your HIV Status and health conditions and have shown Master/Sir (Master's/Sir's name) yours. You both swear to practice sex safely unless otherwise negotiated and if negotiated not to, understand that you are entering into this relationship with the possibility of further infection to each of you. You hereby are actively involved with each other and understand the risks of all sexually transmitted diseases are your responsibilities and shall have no recourse unless otherwise stated here should an infection occur along your journey. You also have agreed upon to the sexual freedom and boundaries established prior to this date and agree to abide by these during the period stated in this contract. You both do this freely and with sound mind and affix your initials below knowing the possible repercussions which may result if you open the relationship and understand there is no recourse if the contracted is altered.

(Write and initial the initials of the parties You also can reinstate the blood and piss exchange as previously discussed in the temporary collaring ceremony to reinforce those with all parties.)

(Back to public)

In the unforeseen event of the death of Master/Sir (Master's/Sir's name) or in the event you decide to revoke this contract, the collar must be removed. In revoking the contract or ending this contract the lock must be smashed and then put into flames for its destruction and a new collar and lock should the boy be further collared? A new contract must be executed to any new Master/Sir or any timetable in accordance with "Old Guard" traditions and ritual to all parties.

Now in keeping of the honor of "Old Guard" tradition, Master/Sir (Master's/Sir's name) please cut your skin and allow the blood to drip. The blood represents the essence of life and what keeps our bodies going and able to move, live, and breathe. It truly is the ultimate sacrifice for our brothers in leather and signifies your permanent relationship with this boy. You Master/Sir (Master's/Sir's name) are responsible for his growth, education and further development of boy (boy's name) not only in leather life but in non-leather life. You also understand that by your dropping of your blood onto your boy's blood, you are sealing this contract and are hereby sealing your commitment to him for the permanent use and service of him as your beloved and indentured servant. The blood that drips on this contract and mixing with your boy's blood is his commitment to you and that together you both seal the promises to live up to together in the commitments that you both have made.

Boy (boy's name), please allow your Master/Sir to cut your skin and allow the blood to drip. The blood represents the essence of life and what keeps our bodies functioning and able to move, live, and breathe. It truly is the ultimate sacrifice for our brothers in leather and signifies your permanent relationship with this Master/Sir (his name) by your dropping of blood on to this contract you boy (boy's name) agree to the permanent collar and acceptance of being in service permanently to him. That you understand and agree to all the conditions and commitments set forth in this contract and will abide by them with your body, mind and soul accepting this dripping of blood as your commitment back to him of your agreement to allow this honor and privilege to begin.

If you both agree please answer, I do.

(Both respond) I do.

You may begin to drip your blood onto the contract.

(They drip the blood at the designated spot with signature below.)

Now while the blood is still flowing, you must press your cuttings together unifying your blood as one and understand that together you are now one in spirit, body, soul and mind and together you will go through life serving your Master/Sir and your Master/Sir being responsible for you totally and unconditionally until the end. Your promise to all the leatherfolk here present as well as family and friends that you understand your commitment and will promise to honor it in "Old Guard" Tradition offering each other the steady, solid, strictness, structure and stability that "Old Guard" upholds and develops without any reservations? You both do this of free mind and spirit and being of sound mind do you understand what you are doing and accept this life together?

(They respond) I do.

Now unite the blood making one life before all your friends, family and leatherfolk here. By doing this now you are honoring one another in life along with the strictness, structure and stability and in the honor of "Old Guard" Traditions and Rituals.

(They press the wounds together then clean up and stop the flow of blood. Again due to HIV and Hep C this portion can be omitted or added as required by the parties. You can also add the piss portion again here and actually piss on to the contract as a symbol of total fluid exchange.)

Everyone here is witnessed to this dripping and comingling of blood (and piss) and sealing of their commitments and agrees to uphold, cherish and guide this new permanent leather family. Everyone here also agrees to honor the right and commitment of this leather family amongst yourselves and the community. To the family, friends and leather tribe here today we all agree to bear witness to the growth of this family, Master/Sir (name) and boy/boi (name) as well as understand what this collar set forth today on this boy's body symbolizes amongst us all. We all have agreed to accept this sealed commitment this date for the lifetime of their lives and by this contract. If you agree may you all please respond saying, I do.

(All respond) I do.

It gives me great honor and privilege to have Master/Sir (Master's/Sir's name) permanently collar his boy (boy's name) this ___ day of (month and year). Please attach the permant collar to your boy and secure the lock.

(Boy is collared and locked)

Master/Sir (Sir's name) you are now the keeper of the key and only in extreme circumstances must the key be released. The circumstance in which the key and collar are to be removed are only for the well-being of the boy and he understands that the key may be given to him only during this time for the removal and reattachment while the well-being is in question. Upon relocking the collar, the key must be returned to his Master/Sir for safe keeping. The collar and lock must be worn at all times and never removed unless for the well-being of this boy only.

To all here I am proud to announce the permanent collaring and commitment of Master/Sir (Master's/Sir's name) and boy (boy's name). May we all honor this commitment from this point forward not only in "Old Guard" traditions and rituals but the protocol now to this family.

You may all congratulate the newly Permanent Collared boy (boy's name) to his Master/Sir (Master's/Sir's name).

This should be written or typed out and all officiating members as well as all the parties should sign including the sponsor. This contract should also be sure to have all dates clearly stated and should be revisited by all within the time span of the contract for furthering of the boy's life as well as any new contracts. Music and other things can be added to make for a larger celebration.

SLAVE COLLAR CEREMONY

TO ALL GATHERED HERE, we are here for the purpose of an official slave collaring ceremony for (slave's name) soon to be known as slave (slave's name) collared to Master (the Master's name). This ceremony is something that the leather tribe looks upon as the commitment of a slave not only sacred, holy as well as a serious commitment. It is also known in "Old Guard" life that our word is our bond! It is intended for a commitment of service with no out, doing only as the Master stipulates in service. It is also recognized that whatever property and belongings this slave owns will become the Master's property for the duration of this slave contract. This commitment also expects the slave to live and serve in Master's Household 24/7/365 in total service and together build one life committed together in service, in leather with all the respect, honor and tradition that "Old Guard" represents as well as the strictness, structure and stability which we uphold in our lives.

I, (Elder's name), as the elder here officiating with (Full name and the position in the club or community as well as the name of the club, community, family) officiate this ceremony in behalf of these two men. (You can have as many official people from many organizations or communities here.) You all are here to bear witness to this slave collaring as the family, friends and leather tribe of these men. With all this said how say you to this serious commitment and responsibility. If you agree you must say I agree.

(All respond) I agree.

Is there any known reason why this Master and slave should not have the ability to have and hold a slave's collar today? If so please state the reason and who is objecting. Otherwise, please remain silent.

(Slight pause for person to speak)

With no response to the first call let us proceed to the second call. Who is sponsoring this slave for collaring and please bring him forth.

(At this time the Master and slave are brought forth. The sponsor is generally well known to the slave. The sponsor represents the original owner of the slave in theory or the slave's family member.)

I, (Elder/Master or head officiator full name) as well as all of you have heard from sponsor of slave. Do you believe he is ready for this collaring? The Master understands the slave is seeking to be owned property and will be trained under this slave collar as well as he accepts the responsibilities of the slave in service and they both accept the responsibility to one another and understand what this commitment of a slave collar means to each other and in leather life. How say all of you? If you believe please answer I believe.

(Everyone else states) I believe.

First are the responsibilities of the Master (should always be Master or higher to own and collar a slave). (State the full name of the Master and the club or community he is from) Do you solemnly swear to abide by the rules of "Old Guard" leather tribe, understanding that your purpose as slave (name of slave) owner, you are responsible for his well-being and mental state as well as understand that the open lines of communication must always be here in order for this commitment in service to you to grow. You understand that the slave collar of this slave means that he is in service to you and you must be responsible not only for his well-being but be his keeper, educator and owner as he continues his leather journey. You understand that in this you are solely responsible for his daily routines. You must agree to owning him in a way that won't violate any of the leatherman's' creeds. R.A.C.K., Safe Sane and Consensual and that each of us walk to our own drummer as he will? Your household must provide a safe environment for him to grow and serve you as well as further his leather life in service. Should you need guidance or assistance in this ownership, you will reach out to your leather brotherhood and ask for help with the understanding it must fit within your guidelines of your household and this contract. You understand that being his owner, you must also understand that you must not abuse your power over your slave to be that of destroying his mental state and not under any circumstance must you ever use physical violence or punishable abuse in his ownership. That financially and emotionally you will support this slave to the best of your ability. The slave collar you hold represents that any person here forward in the leather tribe must ask your permission to touch your slave or have any contact with your slave and without your expressed permission will not be allowed to do so. This is done to protect him under your time as your slave. You also understand that you accept his worldly possessions and property as yours, but you must agree to oversee them only and not dispose or destroy any unless agreed upon by both of you. You are only the keeper of these possessions and property for his well-being not the owner of these possessions and property during his contract to you in service. You also understand that any monies made by your slave he will surrender to you and that you may use these monies for his keep but only with his understanding of what the money is being used for. You do not have the right just to use his money for whatever you want. Again you are only the person who will oversee his spending and savings in accordance with "Old Guard" Tradition. You must agree to take this commitment as serious as any relationship under God and know that you must welcome him to your household with your open heart, mind and body to fulfill his journey as a slave in service to you for the remainder of this slave contract. You promise to stand by him in sickness and in health and for whatever may happen during your time of ownership? You promise to uphold the strictness, structure and stability that is necessary to keep your contract alive and growing in the honor and respect in "Old Guard" traditions and rituals. What say you?

(The Master responds) I do.

slave (name of slave), you understand the from this point forward if you accept this collar having heard your owners responsibilities agree before everyone here that you fully understand these responsibilities set for by your Master and agree to receive these responsibilities and communicate openly with him. You also understand that you are to surrender your worldly possessions and property to him and you agree to allow him to oversee them only and that he will not dispose or destroy any of these possessions and property unless agreed upon by both of you. He is only the keeper of these possessions and property for your well-being not the owner of these possessions and property during your contract to him in service. You also understand that any monies made you will surrender to him and that he may use these monies for your keep but only with your understanding of what the money is being used for. He doesn't have the right just to use your money for whatever he wants. Again he is only the person who will oversee your spending and savings in accordance with "Old Guard" Tradition. You must agree to take this commitment as seriously as any commitment under God and know that you must serve him in your life with your open heart, mind and body to fulfill your journey as a slave in service to him for the remainder of your contract. You promise to stand by him in sickness and in health for richer or poorer and for whatever may happen during your contract of ownership? You also agree that you have signed a separate contract stating all the rules of the household and protocols that you have negotiated with your Master. You agree that both your Master and you understand those negotiated terms. If not, we need to clear them up now. You also agree that you have in your possession those rules of the house, the protocols he wants you to follow and you know completely all that is expected in service prior to signing this contract of ownership. You promise to uphold the strictness, structure and stability that is necessary to keep your commitment alive and growing in the honor and respect to him as well as "Old Guard" Tradition and rituals. What say you?

(slave responds) I do.

That you too will honor the open lines of communication set forth above by your Master. The violation of not honoring this collar and contract with your heart, mind, and body you do realize at that point your slave collar would be removed and the lock destroyed. The punishment of this being considered a total violation of what you have promised here today and you would be released from your duties, responsibilities and your contract of service and your slave collar. The end result would mean you would then have to move out of his home and all educating and mentorship would cease. You also understand that a violation of this sort would cast you out of this community as a breach of your word which is what honor we all stand upon? How say you.

(slave responds) I do.

You must also agree in so taking of this collar, it is the last step in your true "Old Guard" leather journey as a slave and as an owned slave you will also help out in community service and do all that you possibly can do with the other local leather clubs and organizations in service as part of your ownership. That you will serve your Master with all your heart, Mind and Body giving all that you can to achieve what you understand to now be your responsibilities as his owned collared slave. You also agree that you are going to relocate to become a 24/7/365 collared slave under his household and live in his household maintaining his household as soon as feasibly possible.

You understand that as his owned slave you do have the right to openly ask any questions on any order given that you don't understand, but once you understand the directive completely, you will be expected to follow that order as quickly as possible and as effectively as you bodily can. You also agree to accept the continuation of his mentoring, guidance, and education as he set forth in his household and abide by all the rules of the household surrendering yourself physically as the promise to fulfill these requirements. That you will accept punishment when explained what error you made, should you make one, and never use profanity when addressing your Master. You also hereby agree upon relocating, you will actively pursue employment to help aid in the financial keeping of yourself as well as to contribute to the general household finances. You also agree to further your leather education and personal growth as his owned slave being in personal service to your Master.

Slave (slave's name), you do understand that all this is said and done under "Old Guard" rules, traditions and rituals and understand that it is not only an honor but a privileged to be in service to Master (Master's name).

If you understand all what I have said and agree to it what say you.

(slave responds) I do.

You now understand that by agreeing here you will be known as slave (slave's name). Also, that this is a permanent collar and must always be worn except if your life is in jeopardy. If you agree and understand say, I do.

(slave responds) I do.

You do this without any reservations knowing what this slave's collar represents unless violated. If you agree and understand say, I do.

(slave responds) I do.

> Master (his name) and slave (slave's name) understand that on this ___ day ___ year for the period of (insert the period of the contract negotiated contract) this collar must be honored. slave's (slave's name) release of his collar and his position along with all the stipulations in this contract and your slave contract become null and void only in death or violation of his Master (Master's name). If you both agree and understand say, I do.

(Master and slave responds) I do.

(This next part can be private or public depending on the Master and the slave's feelings.)

> slave (slave's name) you are knowledgeable of as of this date to the HIV status and health conditions of Master (Master's name). You also are aware of your HIV Status and health conditions and have shown Master (Master's name) yours. You both swear to practice sex safely unless otherwise negotiated and if negotiated not to, understand that you are entering into this relationship with the possibility of further infection to each of you. You hereby are actively involved with each other and understand the risks of all sexually transmitted diseases are your responsibilities and shall have no recourse unless otherwise stated here should an infection occur along your journey. You also have agreed upon to the sexual freedom and boundaries established prior to this date and agree to abide by these during the period stated in this contract. You both do this freely and with sound mind and affix your initials below knowing the possible repercussions which may result if you open the relationship and understand there is no recourse if the contracted is altered.

(Write and initial the initials of the parties. If the parties want to add the blood and piss portion of the ceremonies previously mentioned they are added here also.)

(Back to public)

> In the unforeseen event of the death of Master (Master's name) or in the event you decide to revoke this contract, the collar must be removed. In revoking the contract or ending this contract the lock must be smashed and then put into flames for its destruction and a new collar and lock should this slave be further collared? A new contract must be executed

to any new Master or any timetable in accordance with "Old Guard" traditions and rituals to all parties.

It now gives me great Honor and privilege to allow you to collar your slave. Master (his name), please collar your slave, slave (slave's name)

(The Master collars his slave)

Now in "Old Guard" Tradition as you, Master (his name), have collared your slave, slave(his name) both understand that together you are now one in spirit, body, soul and mind and together your slave will go through his life serving you, Master(his name). You Master (his name) understand that you are responsible for your slave totally and unconditionally until the end of his contract with you. You, slave (slave name) understand that you have promised to serve only Master solely unless he stipulates otherwise, your life in service to him until the end of your contract to him. You both understand that not only have your done this to each other but in front of all the leatherfolk here present as well as family and friends that you understand your commitments to each other and promise to honor it in "Old Guard" Tradition what you have agreed to today here offering each other the steady, solid, strictness, structure and stability that "Old Guard" upholds and develops in this service relationship without any reservations? You both do this of free mind and spirit and being of sound mind do you understand what you are doing and accept his life in service to you. Master (his name) and your service slave (his name) to Master (his name)? How say you?

(They respond) I do.

Everyone here has witnessed this collaring of this slave and their commitments and agrees to uphold, cherish and guide this new leather family. Everyone here also agrees to honor the right and commitment of this leather family amongst yourselves and the community. To the family, friends and leather tribe here today we all agree to bear witness to the growth of this family Master (his name) and slave (his name) as well as understand what this collar set forth today on this slave's body symbolizes amongst us all. We all have agreed to accept this commitment this date for the (insert period) of their lives and to uphold this contract. If you agree may you all please respond saying I do!

(All respond) I do.

Master (Master's name) you are now the keeper of the key and only in extreme circumstances must the key be released. The circumstance in which the key and collar are to be removed are only for the well being of the slave and he understands that the key may be given to him only during this time for the removal and reattachment while the well being is in question. Upon relocking the collar, the key must be returned to his Master for safe keeping. The collar and lock must be worn at all times and never removed unless for the well being of this slave only.

To all here I am proud to announce the slave collaring and commitment of Master (his name) and slave (slave's name). May we all honor this commitment from this point forward not only in "Old Guard" traditions and rituals but the protocol now to this family.

You may all congratulate the newly collared slave (slave's name) to his Master (Master's name).

This should be written or typed out and all officiating members as well as all the parties should sign including the sponsor. This contract should also be sure to have all dates clearly stated and should be revisited by all within the time span of the contract for furthering of the boy's life as well as any new contracts. Music and other things can be added to make for a larger celebration.

These were only the ceremony parts of a slave collaring. There would be a separate list of protocols and house rules to abide by which would have been signed and negotiated prior to this collaring. This was done so both parties can stipulate anything the two parties wish prior to the signing for both parties to abide by. Anything could be in this slave contract. Also a separate list of belonging and property would have been detailed for all parties to sign and initial so there would be no misunderstanding as to what is whose property after the term of the contract. In a slave contract this was very important as usually a slave was under a contract and usually a slave would move to another Master after the contract and with that his belonging/possessions and properties become part of the value of this slave. It is up to the Master to maintain the integrity of these belongings, property and possession to help with the value of his Slave. As it was back in the old years of slavery, slaves had value and were sold to the next owner. In some "Old Guard" ways this is why all of this was done as to make the slave have value for any owner. In olden days, slaves with no value were passed frequently until such time that they became valuable either through service to their Master or by gaining value to the household so the Master would not want to sell him to the next owner. Here lies the reason why the Master needs to keep the integrity of the slave's possessions, belongings and possessions. The wax, blood and piss portion of the collaring ceremony is optional as a slave is viewed as a possession and property. They are not always looked upon as possible life partners or for a training period. Again it is up to the individuals making the commitments as to what they want added to their particular ceremonies.

NEW AIRPORT PROTOCOLS

With increased security since Sept 11th, airlines in particular have tightened security measures. The amount of goods once allowed in carryon bags has changed drastically.... the Transportation Security Administration Website (www.tsa.gov) gave some basic information:

Carry-on luggage – Prohibited Items – According to Website

- Billy clubs, Bullwhips

- Cattle prods, Hunting knives

- Knives (any length), Martial arts devices

- Metal scissors with pointed tips, Razor blades (not in a cartridge)

- Religious knives, Replica weapons

- SCUBA knives, Sabers

- Straight razors, Stun guns/shocking devices

- Swords, Toy weapons No items that may be used as a weapon or striking implements: Includes:

- Floggers, Wooden paddles

- Leather paddles, Riding crops No restraints of any kind:

- Leather cuffs, Handcuffs (metal or plastic)

- Rope (any length), Chain (any length)

- Arm binders, Straightjackets

No 'sharp' items (or items that can be converted to 'sharp' items):

- Scissors of any type, including EMT scissors No knives, decorative or otherwise

- Marlinspikes (to loosen knots), Needles

- Sabers or swords, CBT toys with spikes

- Whartenburg wheels, Collars with spikes

- Finger knives, or sharpened metal nails, Fur toys with hidden 'nails'

- 'Tweezers' type nipple clamps (rubber ends can be removed)

- No electrical 'stunning' devices: Includes: Violet wands, Electric flyswatters Cattle prods, Tasers

Passengers should be aware that there are no provisions for returning banned items to them when they are left at the security checkpoint. In addition, those who attempt to bring banned items through the checkpoints are subject to civil penalties of up to $1,100 per violation in addition to criminal penalties. So... what CAN you bring in your carry on luggage??

ALLOWED in carry –on luggage:

- Vibrators, Dildos

- Cock rings, Leather clothing including harnesses

- Cock and ball toys (non-spiked), Collars (non-spiked)

- Body paints

- Nipple clamps (clamp type only – not 'tweezers' types)

- Fur toys (except for fur and leather slappers or fur and wooden paddles)

- Needles, IF you have a prescription for them

According to TSA, security checkers have seen their share of sexual objects, and are not shocked or surprised by what they see. If an item is unfamiliar to the guard, the item may be scrutinized at the security check in…so be prepared to answer questions. According to TSA at Portland, the staff does their best NOT to remove items from bags that may be deemed embarrassing… it is not their intent to embarrass customers.

To assist security personnel, put all sex toys into the original boxes and bags that clearly identify what they are…this will help to avoid questions. If you do not have the original packaging, place the items into Ziploc bags with labels on them…this will also speed up the process.

Keep in mind it is normal procedure for random passengers to have their carryon luggage thoroughly searched. During slow times, this may be done away from the gate, in a private area, however, during busy times, it is usually done on a table near the gate, in full view of other passengers, so if you are worried about being embarrassed, don't bring BDSM toys in carryon luggage!

Attitudes

Don't panic If your bag gets tagged for a random check, or if something unusual is spotted inside your bag. Bags get inspected for a number of reasons – usually because something on x-ray was not distinguishable. Beat them to the punch – If you suspect a certain item in your bag is the cause of the problem, discreetly mention the object to security as you pass the security area – then security personnel can make an informed decision. Chances are they will still look in your bag, but they will be able to identify the item quicker.

Be polite and courteous. Chances are the guard will only question the item and it's function then, if it is deemed safe, send you on your way.

Be honest when answering questions. Don't try to make up stories or excuses. It is better to say something is a 'sexual toy' than refuse to answer questions and get in more trouble. Security check sees this stuff every day – it is no big deal to them. You are one person in thousands of strangers. You, and your sex toys, will be forgotten in a matter of minutes.

Answer questions with a hint of humor – quietly let them know you are going to visit a girl or boyfriend you haven't seen in a while – they'll figure out what the 'stuff' is for! But don't overdo the 'humor' – when the x-ray machine beeps, don't loudly declare "OOOPS!! Looks like all my whips and chains set off the machine!" You will quickly find yourself surrounded by armed guards escorting you off to a private area. Be discreet.

Don't cop an attitude if security asks you about something…they are doing their job to keep YOU and everyone on the plane safe. If you feel they have unjustly harassed you regarding an object, quietly move aside, ask to speak to a supervisor, and voice your complaint politely.

If you feel you have been harassed or unfairly treated – if you have some spare time before your flight, or upon your arrival at your destination, call the airport and ask to speak to the Transportation Security Administration office (each airport has one) – they can assist you with your grievance.

If something is considered questionable to security, be prepared to kiss it goodbye. Airports do not 'save' items for later pick-up. Confiscated items are destroyed.

Don't Go Looking For Trouble – don't purposely attempt to carry on items that you know will be confiscated. And don't make a scene if you get tagged for doing so – you end up looking like an ass, it reflects badly on the entire BDSM community – and, worst of all, you will most likely be stuck on a plane with the pissed off people that you held up at the security gate!

One last word on bringing toys on to a plane:

Airline travel is stressful to say the least. Make the flight easier for you – and nicer for the folks you are flying with – by not incorporating play into your travel routine!

Many Dominants like to outfit their subs with metal cock rings, harnesses, etc., under clothing in order to set off metal detectors and 'humiliate' the sub. This may be great for you and your partner, but to the weary business traveler or the harried parents with three whiny children, this is not appreciated.

Games at the metal detector not only slow down other travelers, it causes unnecessary work for airport security. It also makes them non consensual 'partners' in your games.

So do everyone a favor. Play before you leave, and play when you get to your destination. Sitting on a plane with 75 people that you held up at the security gate is not fun!

Checked Luggage – Items Allowed

Toys CAN be packed in checked in luggage – all in the belly of the plane – no access, no worries.

Pack your toys in with your clothes – this will protect them during flight.

Place toys where they can easily be identified. This will speed up the x-ray process and prevent you bag from being pulled and hand searched.

Remove batteries from toys – it doesn't take much jostling of a bag to start a vibrator... and a buzzing bag will draw a lot of attention!

IF you are not overly concerned with airline officials knowing you are kinky, be sure to put your name, address, etc inside the bag in case the luggage tags get lost – this way your bag – and your expensive toys – can be returned.

Bags will be x-rayed, and may be opened if something looks out of the 'ordinary.' but security at checked baggage area expect to see items like knives, sporting equipment, and other unusual items. Bags usually opened only if checkers suspects a possible bomb of some type or if something within the bag is unidentifiable.

But, checked bags are also subject to random searches, so check in toys (and bags) with the understanding that, no matter what, they may be opened and searched. Unless you have undeclared guns or hazardous materials in your bag, it will be passed on to the airplane.

When checking bags, let the check-in personnel know you if have knives or other 'weapons' in your bag – then they can 'tag' your bag for the x-ray personnel and they won't be surprised and feel the need to open and visually inspect your luggage. For further information on procedures for transporting knives, call the airport or the airline you are traveling with.

If you are still worried about traveling with your toys – the best solution:

If you have doubts, pack all items, and have them shipped overnight or next day delivery to your destination hotel. All hotels will receive packages for people who are registered to stay at that hotel – simply call the hotel ahead of time to let them know you are forwarding 'supplies' that you don't want to haul to the airport.

Upon check-in at the hotel, simply have your box delivered to your room.

On the return trip, arrange to have the box sent to your home – your hotel staff can assist you with this.

Airport protocol is something that really isn't "Old Guard" protocol but I have included it here so each and everyone is at least up to date on what is happening now that we travel worldwide and what to expect in an airport with the world as it is today. Since 911 many things even have changed as we travel and it is amazing now that we almost have to ship our toys ahead of time. It is for this reason we need to understand the protocols of today and why they need to be learned. Each Master/Sir boy/boi/submissive/slave should know these and follow them closely so as not to cause attention to themselves in an airport environment. It will save you embarrassment as well as a whole scene at security if you would follow these and update them as they change as the world is changing daily regarding this. I recommend that you keep this handy and make the changes as the changes happen so that the next trip you can make any adjustments to it and have a safe journey.

NEW GUARD VS NEW LEATHER

What is New Guard or New Leather? New Guard is considered people who joined the lifestyle after the computer age. The geneerally are really not into the lifestyle but more about wearing leather. Play leather or pleather, as it was called, is more for the New Guard lifestyle as "Old Guard" was all about real leather and wearing it. "Old Guard was also about BDSM play. Rubber was not included in "Old Guard". Therefore, all of our brothers who wear and enjoy rubber, laytex and all the new fetish gear would be classified New Guard.

The New Leather community as a whole would be accepting of whatever the leather style a person so desires. This now includes rubber men, fetish men of many types of fetishes like laytex, gym clothes, and sports uniforms etc. Many times, people will find their way into New Guard leather life and once accepted begin to find the ways of "Old Guard". Once into leather life they desire to find their way and why they are, what they are. I have to state this that "Old Guard" should not force their ways on New Guard people and new guard should not ignore the traditions and protocols of "Old Guard". They don't have to accept it, but they should never discount the beliefs of the "Old Guard". We all just need to get along with one another as one leather family today. Learn our past for information purposes only, if for no other reason as to why we have changed to where we are today.

"Old Guard" leather claimed many people in the late sixties as we were open to people who didn't belong to any lifestyle and they found their way into leather. Being all accepting of all body shapes made many men feel comfortable. That seemed to be what we became known for. It became why people would find their way to leather life. Due to everyone's different fetishes today New Leather takes each person as they are with all their likes. I believe it was because we were so diverse in our sexual needs in "Old Guard", now people are becoming bored with their vanilla sex lifestyles and are aware of so much more. This is why I believe they try things that New Guard has openly shown. Now they find a place for them to feel at home in New Leather. Once there they generally meet and discover "Old Guard" and the mystique and history it has. Now they can make informed choices of where they want to fit in or at least where we come from.

Many people couldn't find their way, and we as leather folk, helped them do just that. I know I am proud, that as a leatherman, I am open to any person looking, seeking, no matter what the gender, no matter what the fetish; they are welcome in my life. I hold them all as brothers and sisters. I know for me, it has broadened my life tremendously giving me the knowledge of many new things including men becoming women and women becoming men. Leatherfolk now are all accepting and non-judgmental and willing to accept anyone of any shape size or gender into our lives and for that, I as an "Old Guard" Leatherman, am truly grateful.

I know my Master would be proud of it and be proud of me for that. I truly know he would be a supporter, as I knew his beliefs and knowledge as well. We, as leatherfolk, should rally around our brothers and sisters, making us all proud to be whom and what we are. I do also believe that if our brothers and sisters would rally together, celebrating some of these "Old Guard" protocols, rituals and traditions, that our lives would be so much richer and full of great respect for one another. In that, we would make this world a better place to live. I believe we have lost so much respect for one another through time and the deterioration of upholding traditions, that we could all learn something from our elders which would enrich our lives greatly.

Today we are one family. At least we should be. Taking in all the facets of our leather life making us one of the biggest groups in the world. This of course includes the pansexual, bisexual, lesbian and gay communities with all the facets within those communities. We need to help one another and be proud of our leather traditions, ceremonies, rituals, and events and for the good that we do within these communities. Leather folk all over the world now celebrate in this lifestyle, welcoming people from different continents, different cultures, and totally different ways of life to this life of leather. We need to unite and protect and stand tall for all of us.

Master said one day he had hoped to see how big this community would be. Little did he realize where we would be just 30 some years after his death. I know just in my lifetime, I have seen great changes to this life. Some good. Some bad. But whether it's good or bad they have changed the way we are as leatherfolk. We need to be proud and celebrate our achievements and admit to our short comings and try to embrace it all with all the honor and respect that our forefathers had when they began this life. I know it humbles me when I think about it and I realize how far I have come on my journey and I am sure many of you, if you stopped and thought about it, would also be so humbled. Yes it is great and I am proud of who and what I have become. If it wasn't for that "Old Guard" life I wouldn't be who I am. I wouldn't be telling all of you of this experience. Hopefully some of you will listen to my story and understand this as a venture into this new century and what it has to hold. Think about how far we have come and how far we still have to go. I don't think anyone can even embrace all of what we could be. Look at what we have achieved. We still have far to go but I can say I am proud to be a Leatherman in the twenty-first century. I only wished Master could be here. I have something Id like to share with you and that is for you to think about something regarding my life. If he hadn't died on his Motorcycle, where would I be today? If we hadn't lived during that moment of time, would I even be here writing this or If I hadn't met him where would I be?

I know I am so thankful for him and his memories, the "Old Guard" life, the struggles, the gains, the various times of our lives that bring us to this date. That leather breathes and lives in my body in many ways. Hopefully you share in this feeling as leather folk and understand it.

HANKY CODES

Hanky codes were originated in "Old Guard" tradition. They are used to indicate preferred positions and activities by color and placement Left meant dominant/top/Sir/Master and right meant bottom/boy/submissive/slave both indicating what they are into. The left side means being the administrator and the right side being the receiving end. Never in "Old Guard" would you fly both sides in the same town or same evening.

There were originally only four colors in "Old Guard". The original colors were black, grey, yellow and green. As the terms and activities were recognized colors and meanings were assigned. The next color was red and by the early 70's there were many colors recognized. Today the list is endless. Below are some of the most recognized colors and what they mean.

Hanky codes would be next as we near the end of the training. Again this is a time when many new colors are being introduced so this would have to be updated on a regular basis. The ones I have included here in the book are from the latest update I could find and really have added many since the "Old Guard" Times. I believe this will continue to grow and change as we continue to grow and change. It may end up someday having as many colors and fetishes as there are pantone colors in the color wheel. But we must start somewhere and here are the color codes that I would start with. This again is something that wouldn't need to be accomplished right off the bat. It would certainly be an asset to learn and known as time progresses for each individual person. It is something that helps one find their fetishes and also allows everyone in the community to know who and what they are about. I am constantly amazed at some of the colors and fabrics but who am I to judge. I still fly just four basic colors myself and that is black, grey, red and yellow. These are just my preferences. I don't fly one of the original colors and that is green. I don't identify myself as a Daddy. You and your boy/boi/submissive/slave would be free to flag whatever colors you choose and is your right.

WORN ON LEFT	COLOR	WORN ON RIGHT
SM top	**BLACK**	SM bottom
latex fetish top	**CHARCOAL**	latex fetish bottom
bondage top	**GREY**	fit to be tied!
jerk me off	**WHITE**	I'll do us both
fucker	**DARK BLUE**	Fuckee
cop	**MEDIUM BLUE**	Copsucker
pilot/flight attendant	**AIRFORCE BLUE**	likes flyboys
wants head	**LT BLUE**	Cocksucker
69er	**ROBIN'S EGG BLUE**	anything but 69ing
underwater top	**AQUA**	underwater bottom
cock & ball torturer	**TEAL**	cock & ball torture
military top	**OLIVE DRAB**	services military
daddy looking for a son	**HUNTER GREEN**	boy looking for daddy
hustler (for sale)	**KELLY GREEN**	john (looking to buy)
dines off tricks (food)	**LIME GREEN**	dinner plate
spits	**LIGHT YELLOW**	drool crazy
water sports pisser	**YELLOW**	piss freak
two looking for one	**GOLD**	one looking for two
hung 8" or more	**MUSTARD**	size queen
comes in scumbags	**CREAM**	sucks it out

WORN ON LEFT	COLOR	WORN ON RIGHT
two tons o' fun	**APRICOT**	chubby chaser
anything, anytime, anywhere	**ORANGE**	nothing now (just cruising)
suck my toes	**CORAL**	Shrimper
a cowboy	**RUST**	his horse
dildo fucker	**LT PINK**	dildo fuckee
tit torturer	**DARK PINK**	tit torture
fist fucker	**RED**	fist fuckee
2-handed fister	**DARK RED**	2-handed fistee
spanker	**FUSCHIA**	Spankee
cuts	**MAROON**	Bleeds
suck my pits	**MAGENTA**	armpit freak
has navel	**MAUVE**	a navel worshipper
piercer	**PURPLE**	Pierce
likes drag queens	**LAVENDER**	drag queen
smokes cigars	**TAN**	likes cigars
rimmer	**BEIGE**	Rimmee
scat top	**DARK BROWN**	scat bottom
hosting an orgy	**WHTMULTICOLOR DOTS**	looking for an orgy
safe sex top	**BLACKWCHECK**	safe sex bottom
safe fisting top	**RED/HCHECK**	safe fisting bottom

WORN ON LEFT	COLOR	WORN ON RIGHT
milker	**HOLSTEIN**	Milkee
shaver	**RED/WSTRIPE**	Shave
furry bear	**RED/BLACK STRIPE**	likes bears
likes white bottoms	**WHT LACE**	likes white tops
likes black bottoms	**BLACK/ STRIPE**	likes black tops
likes asian bottoms	**YELLOWT STRIPE**	likes asian tops
likes latino bottoms	**BROWN STRIPE**	likes latino tops
sailor	**LT BLUE/ STRIPE**	looking for salty seamen
likes white suckers	**LT BLUE/WHT DOTS**	likes to suck whites
likes black suckers	**LT BLUE/BLK DOTS**	likes to suck blacks
likes asian suckers	**LT BLUE/YELLOW DOTS**	likes to suck Asians
likes latino suckers	**LT BLUE/BROWN DOTS**	likes to suck latinos
park sex top	**RED/ GINGHAM**	park sex bottom
wears boxer shorts	**PAISLEY**	likes boxer shorts
wears kilts	**TARTAN**	checks under kilts
has/takes videos	**BLACK VELVET**	will perform for the camera
voyeur (likes to watch)	**WHITE VELVET**	will put on a show
actually owns a suit	**GREY FLANNEL**	likes men in suits
starfucker	**SILVER LAME**	Celebrity

WORN ON LEFT	COLOR	WORN ON RIGHT
likes muscleboy bottoms	GOLD LAME	likes muscleboy tops
uncut (uncircumsized)	BROWN LACE	likes uncut
cut (circumsized)	BROWN SATIN	likes cut
headmaster	BROWN CORDUROY	Student
likes to nibble	HOUNDSTOOTH	bite me
skinhead top	UNION JACK	skinhead bottom
new in town	CALICO	tourists welcome
has tattoos	LEOPARD	likes tattoos
foot in the hole	RED SOCK	foot fuckee
cuddler	TEDDY BEAR	Cuddle
bestialist top	FUR	bestialist bottom
chicken	KEWPIE DOLL	chicken hawk
wears a dirty jock	DIRTY JOCKSTRAP	sucks it clean
outdoor sex top	MOSQUITO NETTING	outdoor sex bottom
choker	NOOSE	Choke
has drugs	ZIPLOC BAG	looking for drugs
tearoom top (pours)	DOILY	tearoom bottom (drinks)
bartender	COCKTAIL NAPKIN	bar groupie
stinks	KLEENEX	Sniffs

WORN ON LEFT	COLOR	WORN ON RIGHT
mechanic	OILY RAG	in need of a hot oil lube
rides a motorcycle	CHAMOIS	likes bikers
titleholder	STUDDED LEATHER	title chaser
drips hot wax	CANDLESTICK	wicks it up
electrical toys top	EXTENSION CORD	grounding rod
cock pumper	VACUUM CLEANER BAG	wants cock pumped
balloon sex Top	BALLOON	balloon sex bottom
gives enemas	HOSE (NOZZLE)	gets douched
wants to flog	FLOGGER	wants to be flogged
bathhouse top	TERRYCLOTH	bathhouse bottom
top looking for a bottom	KEYS (General)	bottom looking for a top
top wants to take home a bottom	KEYS WORN TOWARD THE FRONT	bottom wants to take home a top
has a home	KEYS WORN DIRECTLY AT SIDE	has a car
top wants to go home with a bottom	KEYS WORN TOWARD THE REAR	bottom wants to go home with a top
needs a place to stay	KEYS IN BACK	looking for a ride
single tonight, come on over	TOOTHBRUSH	lover's in town, your place only

IN CONCLUSION

There have certainly been many changes in leather and SM social life since the late 1950s, but these are more complicated than the simple distinctions between "Old Guard" and "New Guard" can express. Many people today regard just about everything before the 1980s as ""Old Guard"," but by then, leather/SM had already undergone several social revolutions and "Old Guard" was already different from the 1950's and 60's.

Apart from increases in numbers, popularization, and commercialization, the gay leather community has had to deal with one really unique factor that cannot be underestimated: the escalated rate of early mortality due to AIDS. The HIV/AIDS epidemic has damaged leather communities and social life in incalculable ways. Communities have experienced great loss, in a short period of time, of many of the men (and a few women) who made major contributions to creating and sustaining the public leather life we once knew. Now we are facing yet additional epidemics in gay life as a whole. They are Cancer, Crystal Meth and the Hep-C epidemics which again is changing the way we play and the way we in which we share our lives as leatherfolk. People are dying from these epidemics as well and once again the leather community is trying to support and help these individuals. We rally around these individuals offering support both financially and mentally helping them through these new crises as well. It is up to each of us to help our fellow leathermen or leatherwomen in their journeys. Today we need to support them in whatever way we can, infected or not, by any of these epidemics.

The collective absence of so many leather forebears is, I think, one of the main reasons why the social changes of the last decade seem to have produced so much more of a chasm than did previous ones. These people not only built and refined our institutions, but they also met and talked and played with innumerable others, all the while transmitting community values to newcomers. Their loss has damaged the social fabric of the leather community and has created huge gaps in the transmission of leather culture. Some of this culture has been irretrievably lost forever, and our leather society of today has had to reinvent important pieces of itself as a result. For this very reason is why "Old Guard" and New Guard has such differences and now the reason why I have been asked to write about what I witnessed and lived.

Although much has been lost as gay leather/BDSM has evolved, new developments have brought positive changes as well as problems. I'm not proposing that we could or should go back to the 1950s. I also believe we should neither romanticize the past nor fail to value it. Today, there are many ways to acquire leather attitudes and leather knowledge, including open classes, events, books, the internet, structured programs, as well as more valued true traditional apprentice relationships. Many people are realizing we need to value what was good and they are seeking these stories, traditions, ceremonies out and trying to regain the values adding once more the strictness, structure and stability that once was so vital and critical to our way of life. They realize the need and are today trying to reinstate those values and weed out the bad ones but understand why they were there. As well as why we had to change them.

We have only begun to systematically think about our leather history. As more archival and historical material becomes available for study, the stories and details outlined here will undoubtedly be modified. But I suspect that as we read and learn more about our history and why we did what we did, the simple opposition of "Old Guard" and New Guard will be even more radically dislodged by increasingly nuanced and detailed accounts of different leather practices and tribes. The early 1990s resurgence of the loss over "Old Guard" and New Guard ways will itself become a part of our history. The pansexual and lesbians communities desire for all this information as well as many of the gay men's organizations. We are all having classes and seminars, finding their beginnings and history bringing back to life many of the "Old Guard" ways to their New Guard lives.

From a larger perspective, it is clear that there were many differences between "Old Guard" and "New Guard". Overall though, these differences are the differences between life in the US in the 1950s and life now in the 2010s. These differences are common to many groups, not just leather/SM. As the BDSM activity has become popularized, styles have become commercialized, and communities have becomes more open. As this grows, so does the fantasy of "Old Guard" life. What was once a way of life common to many of us leathermen was not a fantasy but a real way of life. People know now there was no one way of life. People seem to like to make up some crazy rules and fantasies about it. What I have documented here was how I lived and breathed and grew into leather life. I hope you will appreciate my journey. I have still kept most of the intimate stories private as they really don't fall under the basics of our lives and hopefully someday soon I will come out with my memoirs which will then be some of the experiences I had in this life. This book is to tell you about the structure, the purpose of it all and why we did it. My journey has some great and hot stories which each of us would probably be able to write about and probably should. You may be surprised as to how they really do simulate one another.

Much of what is described when people talk about changes in the leather community comes down to more people, more money, and more commercialization. Leather public social spaces are less cozy. Communities are now bigger and it's hard to know everyone. People often make judgments about others – and about what is important – based on what they see at a distance on a stage, not what they experience on a daily basis or within the intimacy of a dungeon and the community.

In earlier days, people still had to take risks to be involved in leather/BDSM. There wasn't much to be gained apart from the true experience itself. Today, many people seem to care more about money and their glory. The dream of their high profile, the fancy leathers, the titles of which they represent but really have no knowledge of, than they do about the quality of their interactions. I think we should be more worried about what is happening here than to argue over "Old Guard" vs. New Guard ways. We should all embrace one another for the common goal of the love of leather, the structure it brings to our lives, the stability in which we can embrace our leather lives and the strictness in which we should respect one another on what we have achieved.

Like everything in the years of 2000 plus we have lost so much about who and what we are, but it is about the almighty dollar. "Old Guard" represented the respect and honor of who we were and what we were. It represented the leather journey being that of a poor man or rich man. We were just leathermen all caring about one another, protecting our lives, preserving our rituals and traditions, making us strong as a community, group, and as a person. Now you tell me. Which would you prefer to be part of? I think you will see why leathermen who are of the "Old Guard" Life, cherish and treasure who we are, what we are, and what we stood for. In fact today we still have some "Old Guard" in everyone's life as we still use their titles ie. Master, Sir boy, etc.. So we really haven't lost it all. From these titles come our roots of "Old Guard". If we have these roots why not have others rituals and protocols from the past? If you choose to try "Old Guard" out, I think you will find your life will be sturdier, it certainly will have more structure and the result will give you real stability! The three basic "S's", as I have refered to them of "Old Guard" life.

There are two sayings I would like to have you all think about with this being said. "Try it you might like it" and the last from the famous cereal commercial "Even Mikey Likes it". I think we can all relate to these two sayings.

In my humble way, it has been my Honor and Privilege to share this information with all of you and I thank you for that. I end this book with my usual signature line "Yours In Leather Brotherhood, Master John Ftl".

ABOUT THE AUTHOR

Master John has been actively involved with the BDSM Lifestyle for Over 35 years. He started serving his Master in the true "Old Guard" ways in the Castro in the early 70's. Master John was Honorary Member of the Year 2008 by the South Florida Bondage Club. He was a principle in Daddy's Closet and hosts the website: www.Dungeon Academy.com. He has worked closely with BDSM educators including Jack Mc George, Robert Dante, Catherine Gross, Sebastian, and Pandora. He was the publisher and editor of the Leather Link. He is a past sponsored of the International Leather Sir boy contest regionally and in 2009 and 2010 was a feature theatre presenter and educator. Actively involved in educating our community through Mr. S, LeatherWerks, SFLBC, Leather University, Mens Academy, ILSb, Beyond Leather, S.P.I.C.E., and Leathermen's Academy 2010, his educational focus embraces both gay ad pansexual lifestyles. He is a voting member and contributor to the Leather Archives. He is an experienced judge at many contests globally. Master John co-chairs Leather Title Holders Sunday at the M.C.C. Sunshine Cathedral annually. He is involved in charity work at Tuesday's Angels, Center One, The Leather Masked Ball, Lighthouse for the Blind, The Children with Aids Network, Care Resources, Fort Lauderdale and Hearing from the Heart. Over the past five years, he has attended and presented at more than 200 events. He is an accomplished author and currently just released his book on Cigar Play, "Smoke, Ash and Burning Embers a Handbook on Cigar Play". He currently is the producer of Leathermen's Academy along with his board of directors and holds the Position of President in LMA, Inc. He has traveled extensively as well through Europe.

Printed in Dunstable, United Kingdom